MAGIC MUSHROOMS

COMPLETE GUIDE ON HOW TO GROW AND USE PSILOCYBIN MUSHROOMS SAFELY. DISCOVER THE SECRET FOR CREATING YOUR OWN GARDEN IN THE BEST WAY POSSIBLE

JORGE ED COLEMAN

Table of Contents

Introduction

Hallucinogenic mushrooms are usually included among the list of very dangerous narcotics. These lists, according to David Nutt, a specialist in neuropsychopharmacology at Imperial College London, are an official convention, because there is no direct relationship between the actual classification of drugs and the damage they cause.

According to Nutt, the reality is that many narcotics treated as taboo are not as harmful to the consumer as compared to other drugs that pose significant health risks such as heroin, crack, methamphetamine, cocaine or alcohol.

The two studies on psilocybin come to light a few days after the "US Food and Drug Administration" approved a series of experiments with ecstasy, to study their therapeutic possibilities in patients affected by post-traumatic stress disorder.

Already in the 60s, LSD, ecstasy or psilocybin offered, for many psychiatrists, new and exciting medical perspectives. The strict anti-narcotic laws that emerged, however, during the 1970s were an obstacle to investigations. Scientists interested in their possibilities have since had to fight against legal, ethical and cultural difficulties to reopen options for experimenting with them.

The therapeutic use of psilocybin is nothing new. In different cultures, traditional medicine has used them to heal. From the

Aztec civilization, through the popular María Sabina in Mexico, even healers of the same Iberian Peninsula just 20 years ago, according to a study by Juan Andrés Oria de Rueda, professor of mycology at the University of Valladolid, in which he has collected testimonies of older women who in the past trained as healers in Extremadura, Ávila and Zamora.

"These types of fungi have been used primarily for headaches, these are widespread native species in Spain, such as the Psilocybe semilanceata, to those who called Fungueiru or Mushroom of Aunt Juana, and who are very present in grassland areas, because they grow mainly thanks to the droppings of cattle", Oria de Rueda explains to VICE News. "His interest is to try them for treating cluster migraines, which are headaches so intense that there have even been cases in which they have led to suicide", explains Oria.

Amanita muscaria, which contains other hallucinogenic substances, such as muscimol and ibotenic acid "are the best known, but have different effects", Oria points out.

Psychedelic substances, both LSD and psilocybin, were used in clinical psychiatry research until after 1971, after United Nations Convention on Psychotropic Substances, they were gradually banned worldwide, James Rucker, a specialist tells VICE News.

Psilocybin can reconfigure the brains of people with depression and eliminate the loop of negative thoughts.

This British psychiatrist defends the need to give more facilities permission to research with these substances, to the point that he has made a banner by publishing the prestigious British Medical Journal, with an article in which he asks for the requalification of these substances for scientific use.

He's not the only one. David Nutt, who has suffered a long bureaucratic path to get to do his clinical trials to treat depression, has also published another report article in PLOS Biology this year. He has found it very difficult to obtain the necessary permits by the European Union and the British government. He also denounces the control of the sale of psilocybin by the only laboratory that produces it.

Chapter 1 History Of A Magic Mushrooms

As mentioned in the history of mushrooms, some mushrooms have been used for religious purposes and in different rituals. These mushrooms, which have been of great importance according to a religious point of view, are mostly Psilocybin mushrooms. These mind-catching bodies have been an important part of cultures deprived of time and space. Many religions and philosophies of the world have been influenced by these "Magic Mushrooms."

Reko, Richard E. Schultes, Roger Heim, and R. Gordon Wasson are the lucky scientists and researchers who are responsible to re-discover the remains of ancient usage of Psilocybin mushrooms. They discovered that the old native Mesoamerican people used Psilocybin mushrooms in their rituals and ceremonies. Their research showed that modern-day mushroom cultures have ancestral links with the Psilocybin mushrooms, which were used in the religious practices of some civilizations like Aztec and Mayan. The cultural roles played by Psilocybin mushrooms in ancient times are depicted by the old rocks and stones containing Psilocybin mushroom pictures, discovered from the ruin of Mayan temple. History shows that the Aztec people had too much belief on a specific Psilocybin mushroom (Psilocybe Mexicana) that they name it Teonanacatl, which means "God's Flesh." A Franciscan in the 16th century went on an expedition with a team and reported about the beliefs of Aztec about "God's Flesh," but misguided Catholics. Catholics were running a campaign against Paganism at that time, and they were misguided about the usage of mushrooms. They restrict the use of Psilocybin mushrooms as they thought that Pagans worship these mushrooms. This all resulted in the planned demise of this culture, but they couldn't destroy some evidence. The research and reports by Franciscan Bernardino De Sahagun is the ultimate source of knowledge about usage of Psilocybin mushrooms by Aztec tribes.

Further Improvement in the Discovery of Psilocybin Mushrooms

This situation gave rise to a new belief, with a mix of Christianity and mushroom rituals. R. Gordon Wasson and his team also discovered an indigenous healer named Maria Sabina, who practiced the use of Psilocybin mushrooms to heal many mental, physical, and spiritual problems. People said that she had specific "Magic Mushrooms." In search of Magic mushrooms, the people of America came to know about the Psilocybin mushrooms of Mexico. When more people came to know about Maria Sabina, her popularity reached out of America, and many people searched for her due to her magical mushrooms. Not only in Mexico and America, but the traditional and religious use of Psilocybin mushrooms had also been found in ancient European culture. The philosophers Aristotle, Plato, Homer, and

Sophocles, were seen in history, participating in the ceremonies in a different temple Demeter, in front of the goddess of agriculture. Strange types of ceremonies were used to be held in those temples where people believed that they got changed after spending a night there. A conference about mushrooms was held in 1977 in Europe in which different psychoactive mushrooms of the world were discussed, and researchers got a new thing to research on.

Wasson and his team were the first Ethnomycologists, while Jonathan and his team proved themselves to be the second generation of Ethnomycologists. Human history has dramatic effects of Psilocybin mushrooms and many more yet to come. If we talk about the history of natural cultivation of Psilocybin mushrooms, A French mycologist Roger Heim was the pioneer who cultivated many Psilocybin species successfully, in the 1950s. He used the materials which were brought by Wasson and his team from their journey. Then the work started, and many Psilocybin mushroom species were discovered till the end of 1970s, and still there are many mushrooms yet to be discovered.

History Of Mushroom Cultivation

The cultivation of Mushrooms was started back in 600s, in Asia. But in Europe, the fungus cultivation (specifically mushrooms) was started in the 1600s. History shows that the cultivation of Mushrooms in Paris was started in the 1650s when a native farmer saw growing fungus in his field of Melons. He then thought to cultivate this fungus on a commercial level, and this was the time to change thoughts about mushrooms. He delivered this umbrella-shaped fungus to restaurants where it was used as a dish. That type of mushrooms was named "Parisian Mushroom."

Researchers found fungus growing in caves around Paris, whose history dates back in the 1600s when French gardeners found that the humid and cool environment of caves is suitable for mushroom cultivation. Therefore mushrooms were cultivated at large scale in caves. In the Netherlands, mushrooms were introduced for cultivation in the 1800s but in small scales. Then after some time, large scale cultivation of mushrooms was done in marl mines in Limburg. After caves and mines, other methods of mushroom cultivation were developed, which then resulted in high mushroom yields in the region. Before that, mushrooms were specific, and they were only available for elites. Dutch people had the most strict rules for mushroom cultivation, and they had their own specific controls over the cultivation. That was the reason that the Netherlands became the largest mushroom producing country 50 years ago. But then, Chinaand the USA came into the competition of mushroom cultivation. China produces about 70% of the world's mushrooms now, so China is at the first position in mushroom cultivation, and then comes the USA and Netherlands.

Chapter 2 What Are Psilocybin Or Magic Mushrooms

Psilocybin is a psychedelic drug that works by enacting serotonin receptors, most often in the prefrontal cortex. This part of the brain influences mood, discernment, and perception.

Psychedelic drugs work in other regions of the brain that regulate arousal and panic reactions. Psilocybin doesn't always cause active visual or auditory hallucinations. Instead, it mutilates how some people that use the tranquilize perceive objects and people already in their condition.

The quantity of the medicate, past experiences, and expectations of how the experience will take shape can all impact the effects of psilocybin.

After the gut ingests and consumes psilocybin, the body converts it to psilocybin. The hallucinogenic impacts of psilocybin usually happen within 30 minutes of ingestion and last between 4 and 6 hours.

In some individuals, the changes in sensory recognition and the underlying patterns of thoughts can last for a very long time.

Psilocybin containing Mushrooms is usually tan, brown, and small, and they are often regarded by some people in the wild as botch mushrooms containing psilocybin for any number of other mushrooms that are poisonous.

People ordinarily consume psilocybin as a fermented tea or prepare it with nourishment to veil its unpleasant taste in the mouth. Dried Mushrooms are crushed by manufacturers into powders and prepared in capsule forms, while some specific people consume these mushrooms meal with chocolate.

Psilocybin is delegated a Schedule I tranquilize, which means that it has a high potential for misuse and has no currently accepted therapeutic use in treatment in the United States.

Although certain societies have known to use the stimulating properties of some mushrooms for centuries, psilocybin was first secluded in 1958 by Dr. Albert Hofmann, who likewise discovered lysergic corrosive diethylamide (LSD).

Therapeutic Use

In the material above, I've offered some details as to how psilocybin and psychedelics, in general, can be used therapeutically. Testing of psilocybin by the medical community is still in its infancy, as laws have only begun to allow limited investigation within the last decade. The medical community is currently exploring its medical uses for a number of conditions. These include depression, addiction, PTSD, cluster headaches and migraines, OCD, and mood and anxiety disorders. Results thus far have been promising in each of these areas.

It's worth mentioning that initial results suggest psilocybin is far more effective in the treatment of depression than anything currently accepted for medical use. Results come more quickly and tend to be longer lasting than other drugs on the market. In addition, unlike these other drugs, patients using psilocybin for treatment of depression do not need to be continuously medicated for the treatment to be effective. In addition, initial research into the use of psilocybin treatment for addiction is more promising by far than any form of treatment thus far discovered.

Psilocybin also has great potential for emotional healing. PTSD and mood and anxiety disorder are just a few of the conditions that have been responsive to psilocybin therapy. Similar studies have shown that psilocybin has been effective at significantly reducing the emotional pain associated with social rejection.

There is no doubt that further studies will show the profound benefits of psilocybin and other psychedelics for treating trauma and all forms of emotional healing. Given the deep impact of emotion on every aspect of our lives, this suggests that psychedelics may be the single most powerful healing tool available to us.

It's noteworthy that a new research division has recently been set up and funded in the Psychiatric Department of the John Hopkins Hospital in the USA, specifically to look at the potential therapeutic effects of psychedelics–and especially psilocybin mushrooms and cannabis.

In the meantime, some relatively recent research undertaken by Dr Griffiths et al from John Hopkins University[2], is interesting and may provide some guidelines about the dosages you choose for yourself. This research helps to explain why, although it is impossible to overdose on mushrooms from a toxicity point of view and they are not addictive, it is necessary to exercise caution because of the intensity of the effects you may experience.

Griffiths et al were looking at possible therapeutic uses for psilocybin, especially for depression and PTSD, in view of its reported long-term positive effects.

They administered varying strengths of psilocybin to 30 volunteers in one study and followed it up with a similar study with 18 volunteers a few years later. They used dosages of 5, 10, 20 and 30mg psilocybin per 70kg body weight of the volunteer, administered either in increasing or decreasing dosages, and at a rate of about once per month. On average this would translate to about 0.8g, 1.6g, 3.2g and 4.8g of dried P cubensis (and matches our description of light, medium, strong and "heroic" doses given earlier).

Some of their findings are useful:

Doses of 20mg and 30mg produced a mystical experience for 72% of the group (this would be 3.2g and 4.8g in our P. cubensis calculation).

One month and even 14 months after these higher dosages, participants rated the experience as having had noteworthy personal and spiritual significance. Up to 65% also reported sustained positive changes in attitude, mood and behavior after 30mg. The 20mg group had similar results, with 60% reporting sustained positive changes.

Those who had had the ascending doses (i.e. starting low and getting stronger) reported the most positive results. This result was not the same as other research, which suggests that an immediate very strong experience might have long-term positive therapeutic results.

Those who monitored and recorded the sessions observed that most reactions increased with the increasing dosage[3]. For example, the chance of the participant crying increased with the dosage; arousal, distance from ordinary reality and happiness were highest at the 30mg dosage. However, interestingly, the highest level of peace/harmony was at the 20mg level.

Also, the researchers found that the 30mg dose gave rise to some unpleasant outcomes.

It was the only level where monitors reported significant paranoid thinking.

86% of the participants experienced extreme fearfulness, and an average time of about 11 minutes of strong anxiety. By comparison, at the 20mg level, only 14% experienced extreme fearfulness, with only 2 minutes of extreme anxiety. At 10mg, there was no fearfulness and only 1 minute of strong anxiety.

So, it would seem wise to start with low dosages, with 20mg being the most effective and carefully consider your chances of having a bad trip if you try very high dosages.

Personal Growth

While therapeutic benefits focus more on the use of psilocybin and other psychedelic compounds for healing, there may be huge benefits for healthy individuals as well. This is an exciting area of study, as it may provide a key for enhancing our capacity for healthy functioning on numerous levels. Therapeutic studies suggest that psilocybin can reduce the impact of negative states like social anxiety, distraction, and lack of motivation. At the same time, positive mental resources like creativity, cognitive function, and productivity have been enhanced through psilocybin use.

On a biological level, psilocybin has been shown to stimulate the growth of new brain cells and facilitate learning. Psilocin, the bioactive metabolite of psilocybin, stimulates the 5-HT2A serotonin receptors in the prefrontal cortex. This has two immediate biological effects. The first is an increased production of Brain Derived Neurotropic Factor (BDNF). Essentially, this stimulates the growth of neurons and neural connections and the activity of these neurons. At the same time, the brain produces more glutamate, a neurotransmitter responsible for learning, memory, and cognition.

With regard to global brain function, psilocybin dampens the activity of the Default Mode Network (DMN). This is a portion of the brain associated with a variety of mental activities including self-reflection, daydreaming, and thoughts of the past or future. When the activity of the DMN is dampened, it is easier for the brain to form new and different neural connections. This means learning new activities and information.

To put this into perspective, consider the act of concentration. Effective concentration requires present moment awareness. Thoughts of the past or future, excessive self-reflection, and daydreaming are dilutions of present moment awareness. They are processes that interfere with present moment awareness. Though these activities have their place, the DMN is often overactive, resulting in excessive self-analysis and counterproductive attention to memories or future possibilities. When the DMN has the volume turned down, the mind becomes more capable of focus and concentration, allowing us to be more productive and to learn new things more quickly and effectively.

Psilocybin also increases global neural function. In typical waking states, many parts of the brain operate more or less independently from one another. Psilocybin causes these parts of the brain to synchronize with one another, allowing more of the brain to operate as a whole rather than a collection of parts.

The communication between these various regions is strengthened, and the linkages formed during the trip tend to persist even after the psychedelic experience has ended. In the process, the brain is "rebooted." It is reprogrammed and the neural activity is significantly reorganized.

Despite the advances of medical science, we still know very little about the brain compared to what is left to be discovered. Because of this, we cannot conclusively determine the impact of this reorganization. However, anecdotal evidence suggests that it is linked to greater empathy and compassion, higher levels of creativity and innovative thought, and the capacity to overcome fear-based blockages. These are just a few of the most profound and oft-cited results that have been described in the bulk of those who have used psilocybin.

As mentioned above, this is a subject that can be discussed extensively, and this book is dedicated more to safe use and psilocybin mushroom cultivation. However, before moving on, it is worthwhile to mention that moderate doses of psilocybin have been shown to shift the brain waves to the alpha rhythm, a state observed in both meditation and flow states. Higher doses have been linked to a dissolution of the ego, which, in turn, provides an opportunity to restructure our perception of ourselves and the world.

Microdosing

The use of psilocybin mushrooms and other psychedelics has historically been linked to powerful hallucinogenic experiences. Early research focused on the potential of psychedelics to induce mind-expanding spiritual experiences. These experiences were based on the capacity of large doses of psychedelic compounds to elicit profound changes in the perception of reality. However, in recent years, the practice of microdosing has been gaining attention. This involves the use of psychedelics to gain cognitive benefits without entering a full-blown trip.

Microdosing has, to some extent, increased the legitimacy of psychedelic use. One reason for this is that it is becoming popular among professionals in competitive industries such as those in Silicon Valley. By using a small amount of psilocybin or other psychedelic compounds, professionals are able to gain a competitive edge. Microdosing can help a user to increase creativity and productivity while reducing the effects of anxiety and depression. Furthermore, this is a practice that can have lasting benefits, even after the regimen has been completed.

Essentially, microdosing is exactly what it sounds like. When on a psilocybin mushroom microdosing regimen, a user will ingest a small, measured dose of psilocybin mushrooms. The effect is sub-perceptual, meaning that it is below the amount needed for a psychedelic experience. After ingestion, the user will then go about work or their regular routine just as they would under normal circumstances.

Though the psychological effects are subtle, the benefits can still be profound. They include improved energy levels, problem-solving capacity, and focus.

Chapter 3 The Structure of Mushrooms

This chapter will go into greater detail regarding the physiology of a mushroom trip, namely how the chemical compounds affect the brain and what sensory or perceptual changes we experience while affected.

A psilocybin mushroom is part of a group of polyphyletic (poly-phil-eh-tick) fungi. Meaning these organisms are grouped together scientifically due to their structure and chemical makeup but share no common ancestor. These organisms contain various psychedelic compounds (in various quantities), such as psilocybin (sil-OH-sigh-bin), psilocin (silo-OH-sin), and (in minor degrees) baeocystin (bay-OH-cyst-in).

Psilocybin is the main psychoactive compound in magic mushrooms. Once ingested, this compound is converted to psilocin. While psilocin is already present in the mushroom, it is in much smaller amounts and degrades much faster outside the human body.

The conversion of psilocybin to psilocin happens in the digestive tract, which makes other methods of use not nearly as effective as ingestion. Both psilocybin and psilocin are structurally similar to serotonin (known chemically as 5-hydroxytryptamine or 5-HT), mimicking it in the human brain, allowing it to bind with it, causing similar changes.

Serotonin is an important neurotransmitter in the human brain which is responsible for regulating mood and social behaviors. It acts as a message delivery system between nerve cells. Since serotonin affects mood, drugs that affect the uptake of serotonin (such as psychedelics) have been used in research for the treatment of mood disorders (McIntosh, 2018) as well as the treatment of migraines and a variety of chemical addictions (Price & Brown, 2019).

Psilocin is relatively unstable and in the presence of oxygen it will present blue or black as it degrades. You can see this when you tear the meat of one of these mushrooms in half. It will react especially well in alkaline conditions and will change immediately. It is also the reason why mushrooms containing the psilocin compound bruise easily when picked. Luckily, the amounts of psilocin are negligible and thus the degradation thereof does not have much effect on the potency of the mushroom. With the stability of psilocybin as compared to psilocin, the former is the preferred compound for use during research.

Additionally, psilocin interacts with serotonin and all its receptor subtypes. It mimics the effects of these neurotransmitters, except dopamine, which potentially boosts their effectiveness. While hallucinogens do react with these receptors and various subtypes, so far, none have been definitively identified as the main reactor to psychedelic compounds.

Psychedelic mushrooms have a lot in common with LSD, also known as acid (a synthesized version of psilocybin created by Albert Hoffman). They have similar effects on the body, with both acting on the central nervous system, distorting perceptions.

Unlike the popular misconceptions, both psychedelic mushrooms and LSD do not create hallucinations, nor induce visions of things that do not exist. They simply distort and/or enhance what is already there.

The overall behavioral effects of consuming psychedelic mushrooms depend completely on each individual and personal sensitivity to the compounds found in the mushrooms. Other factors such as previous experiences, setting, and present mood also affect the behavior and perceived effect of mushrooms. Further, it is important to note that even experiences within the same individual can vary from dose to dose, not just between different people.

For the most part, the physical effects are not overly significant. There have been some reports of pronounced and persistent adverse effects such as muscle aches, shivering, and elevated blood-pressure. However, that could be attributed to compound sensitivity or a case of misidentification of the species of mushroom.

While body temperature generally stays constant, other negative effects include abdominal pain, nausea and vomiting, and an increase in heart rate. All of which could be detrimental if not checked, or monitored, especially if someone ingests mushrooms in conjunction with other medications for established conditions (European Monitoring Center for Drugs and Drug Addiction, 2018).

In addition to the aforementioned, a significant physiological effect is pupil dilation. Increased levels of serotonin in the brain causes this effect. As psilocybin is interlinked with the uptake and production of serotonin, naturally your pupils will dilate when using psilocybin or its derivatives.

Normally, pupils dilate or constrict in response to changing light levels. The lower the available light, the larger our pupils get. This is called dilation. However, other factors such as intense sexual interest, complex cognitive tasks (think solving a seriously complicated mathematical equation) or ingesting certain drugs or medications will dilate pupils as well.

Pupil dilation or mydriasis (my-dry-uh-sis) happens when certain muscle groups in the eye are activated. The two groups responsible for this are the iris sphincter and dilator. These two muscle groups are triggered by different inputs.

The iris sphincter muscles are connected and affected by our automated bodily functions. What this means is that these muscle groups control whenever the doctor shines a light in your eyes or when you focus on items at varying distances from you.

The iris dilator is directly linked to the human flight-or-fight response. It is most notably affected by dopamine instead of serotonin, which affects adrenaline in the human body. Needless to say, psychedelics or other psychoactive drugs will have a great effect on both of these muscle groups.

Therefore, depending on the type of drug and which neurotransmitter is affected, either group can be activated. Drugs that affect these neural pathways (and even adrenal glands) will often also affect the physiological response as well.

Drugs that affect serotonin levels (not just psychedelics) such as ecstasy, cocaine, and amphetamines will increase these levels. The result of triggering the increase in neurotransmitters is the physiological response of pupil dilation. It is interesting to note that there are some medicines, such as antidepressants, that also affect serotonin and so will also affect pupil dilation.

Consequently, this will also present in individuals that are exposed to psychedelics, such as LSD or magic mushrooms. The larger the spike in serotonin, the higher the chance of inducing a psychedelic episode as described above.

Drugs that affect the production of dopamine, such as cannabis, or that affect the adrenal glands in any way will also trigger the physiological response of mydriasis. However, they will have other physiological effects that may or may not coincide with the release of increased serotonin and related effects.

It is also important to note that not all drugs or medications will affect dilation to the same degree. Ecstasy will produce a larger response as compared to antidepressants. Opiates, on the other hand will have an opposite effect, constricting the muscle groups instead of dilating them. Combining different drugs that produce different physiological effects will present this response in varying degrees (Dvorsky, 2015).

Accompanying the physiological effects, there are a host of other sensory distortions as well. Since they vary in intensity from person to person and trip to trip, these kinds of experiences are entirely subjective. The effects include, but are not limited to, feelings of euphoria, giddiness, joy, and a greater sense of relaxation. Existing textures and tastes could be enhanced or changed in several ways.

Some individuals report distortions of their perception of time, stating that time felt stretched or compressed or twisted in different ways (Brodwin, 2016). Another linked side-effect of this time-distortion is the feeling of being separated from the self in a way such as an out of body experience.

The individual could experience visual distortions in the form of brighter colors, waves, ripples, warped surfaces or images, and the appearance of images within those patterns. While there are some reports of individuals who insist that they had experiences seeing things that did not exist, the most likely explanation would be their brain's interpretation of the visual distortions they experienced while on the trip.

There has been research done to map the neural pathways of the brain of people given the drug (and a placebo used as a control) in order to determine how it affects these pathways. Researchers noted stronger activity across several regions in the brain which had not displayed in the control groups (Brodwin, 2016).

Unfortunately, these experiences are not all enjoyable and could turn sour in an instant. Termed as a "bad trip," these sudden negative distortions could warp the emotional experiences and cause enhanced feelings of anxiety (lasting anywhere from 30 minutes to hours after the fact) that can only be relieved (and in some cases reduced) after the drug has worn off. Other effects include depression and the possibility of inducing episodes of various psychoses.

However, in a 2012 study headed by David Nutt, researchers have found that additional changes in brain activity causing hallucinations of those that were given doses of psilocybin, could be the key to understanding how depression works in the brain and how magic mushrooms could ease these mental disorders (Carhart-Hariss et. al., 2012).

The study showed that people who suffer from depression have over connected pathways in their brains that cause intense feelings of negativity. Taking the drug showed muted activity in these areas of the brain, leading Nutt to believe that controlled use of psilocybin mushrooms could ease depression and other mental illnesses.

Therapy

There are still many ongoing clinical trials regarding the therapeutic and medical use of psilocybin, including research conducted to see if psilocybin and its derivatives could be used to reduce addiction and drug dependency in individuals (Sessa, 2018).

Even though there are past trials that have evidence to support the theories that magic mushrooms have healing properties and therapeutic benefits (Hoffman, 2016) the majority of these studies have focused their efforts mainly on the effect psilocybin has on psychological disorders (Boseley, 2016).

The main psychoactive effects of psilocybin mushrooms are attributed to psilocybin and psilocin compounds found within the mushrooms. When psilocybin is broken down in the intestinal tract, it gets converted to psilocin. This chemical reaction and breakdown that occurs followed by the uptake of psilocin is what causes the psychedelic effects as it acts upon the brain.

However, it is important to note that use in a controlled setting reduces the risk of aggravating existing disorders. Combining psilocybin mushrooms with other drugs or compounds is ill advised as they could interact in undesirable and often unpredictable ways.

The body creates a resistance to these compounds, however, making it incredibly difficult to abuse the drug. This means that the shorter the amount of time between doses, the less effective the drug becomes. So far there has been no definitive proof that the substance causes physical or psychological dependencies (van Amsterdam, 2011).

That being said, it could still be easy to keep taking the drug, and up your dosage in order to get that "high." Meaning that, should you ingest psilocybin soon after the previous dose, you would need to increase the dose in order to have the same effect as the previous one (Mush Planet, n.d.).

While not at all common, an overdose is still a possibility, especially if doses are not measured carefully for your body weight and desired effect. Unlike other drugs, an overdose on psilocybin mushrooms does not have a physical effect that is as easily discernible from a general bad reaction.

While overdosing is practically impossible if proper dosage instructions are followed, mushrooms can cause severe nausea, abdominal pain, diarrhea, and seizures that could result in a coma and death.

An average dose for a person weighing 140 pounds (65 kilograms) is 1.9 grams of dried product (0.03 ounces). The important part here to take note of is that measuring in grams is the preferred (and more accurate) way in order to control the dosages (Zamnesia, n.d.).

It does also have serious (and often dangerous) mental ramifications:

- Intense panic attacks coupled with a prolonged trip.
- Feelings of losing control.
- Extreme paranoia and delusions leading to psychosis or psychotic episodes, regardless of existing mental disorders.
- In very rare cases, an overdose will cause a complete psychological collapse, often leading to the individual needing to be hospitalized (Miller, 2019).

A lot of the negative side-effects that are attributed to ingesting psilocybin mushrooms come from improper growth and crop care.

Many other symptoms, such as nausea, vomiting, muscle weakness, incoordination, and drowsiness are the result of contamination from other spores and mold due to improper care being taken while handling the mushrooms during growth or preparation.

Accidentally inhaling spores could also have a negative effect similar to those conversed above and beyond the following:

- Runny nose, sneezing fits.
- Tightness in chest, wheezing.
- Asthma attacks.
- Increased susceptibility to allergic reactions.

Below are some effects, mental and physical, to be expected following the ingestion of psilocybin mushrooms:

- Enhancement of emotions.
- Hallucinations, as well as both colors and music are experienced more intensely.
- Distortion of the sense of reality.
- Loss of sense of time.
- A spiritual sense of understanding.
- Ecstasy, arousal, and excitement often combined with uncontrolled outbursts laughter.
- Fear, bewilderment, and anxiety.
- An increase in body temperature, heart rate, and blood pressure.

• Nausea, diarrhea, dizziness, and trembling.

There are also reports from individuals citing persistent perception distortions (visual, auditory, etc.) that would last up to months after the last dose (van Amsterdam, 2011).

Once ingested, the mind-altering effects last from three to eight hours. The first three hours typically being the peak of the experience. In this time, the majority of symptoms or effects can be observed (Wikipedia, 2019).

Some of these distortions appeared as soon as 30 minutes after taking the first dose, but only becoming undeniably noticeable at the two-hour mark.

Much like other psychedelics, the setting plays a major role in how successful or enjoyable an individual's experience will be. Since psilocybin mushrooms and other psychedelics enhance emotions and moods, rather than creating them, the setting is of utmost importance.

It is also highly recommended (for both those that are new to mushrooms as well as those who already have some experience) that the individual needs to be accompanied by a trusted friend or someone who knows what to expect. If you are able to ground yourself in an environment that elicits comfort and safety, your experience is more likely to be a good one (Wikipedia, 2019).

The setting refers to the environment you will be in during the time you ingest psilocybin mushrooms. An environment that is inherently negative or uncomfortable will enhance the negativity of the experience.

While you could do everything possible to make the experience as beneficial to you as possible, feelings of depression, anxiety, and/or lack of concentration are common alongside the feelings of euphoria and relaxation.

An important note: If you are going to harvest from the wild, the risk of misidentification is high, which could result in poisoning yourself and/or others. Many of the safe, psilocybin varieties are easily mixed up with poisonous mushrooms due to similarities in appearance and initial bodily response. However, these mushrooms can lead to severe illness and even death.

Most mushrooms have the same basic physical appearance. Walk down the produce aisle in any grocery store and 9 times out of 10 you will find mushrooms washed and neatly packaged, ready for use. However, these mushrooms are mostly just the cap or a small part of the stem.

The mushroom, cap and stem included, is known as the fruit of the organism. This is generally the part that is eaten.

The cap is the hat, or umbrella-shaped clump at the top of the mushroom. Directly underneath the cap is a membrane known as a veil (different from the universal veil as described below). This thin, papery “skin” protects the gills, or pores, that lie between it and the cap. Within these gills is where the organism produces and stores spores. The stem (stipe or stalk) is the rubbery, fibrous part of the organism that supports the cap (or the hat) that transports nutrients for growth.

At the bottom of the stem is the volva. Also known as the universal veil. This is the membrane that covers the immature mushroom and keeps it protected. It tears as the stem grows stronger and taller. It can take on the appearance of a cup or a cocoon out of which the stem grows. Below the volva grows the mycelium. Within the mycelium is the hairy "roots," known as hyphae, that transform the substrate into fuel for the organism so that it can grow.

Chapter 4 Effects and Risks Of Psilocybin Mushrooms

The most important chemical compound in this mushroom actually influences the levels of serotonin in the human mind, causing visual and mental distortions. The effects last as long as the body needs to metabolize the compound, which can take up to six hours.

Aside from the type of mushroom that determines its potency and the dosage that determines the amount of the hallucinogen that you'll take, the nature and intensity of experience are greatly affected by your own state of mind, environment, and mental health.

On the downside, there are also reports of mushrooms causing severe hallucinations and psychological experiences that can worsen already existing mental conditions. This experience is known as a "bad trip." A bad trip happens if an overly high dosage is taken, or if the psychoactive substances inside the mushrooms react with other medications that you are currently using.

Caution is advised when taking any psychoactive substance, particularly hallucinogens. They have the potential to trigger numerous mental symptoms and problems, which can cause life-threatening behaviors and accidents. While this is a theoretical possibility, there have been little to none known accidents or deadly outcomes reported due to the use of psychoactive mushrooms.

There's a lot of variations when it comes to mushroom potency and the amount of psychoactive substances that they contain. This is close to impossible to determine as the potency doesn't only vary depending on the species but also the environment in which they were cultivated.

For this reason, it's not uncommon for mushrooms to induce a wider range of responses from nausea, sleepiness, dizziness, a weakness in muscles, to even disturbed coordination, and strong headaches.

When it comes to mental effects, magic mushrooms can induce positive experiences like spiritual insights and a changed perception of reality, time, and space. However, they can also cause intense paranoia and nervousness that can become so intense it can initiate panic attacks or even psychosis. While this book will present you with research that confirms the possible benefits of using psychedelic mushrooms for long-term use, negative outcomes have also been reported, such as personality changes and the development of flashbacks.

There are many health risks that can occur if you take magic mushrooms without sufficient knowledge and caution. It's always possible for psychedelic mushrooms to be confused with non-edible mushrooms, or even poisonous ones. This increases the risk of poisoning. Another important safety risk to consider is the possibility of confusing the fly agaric mushrooms with psilocybin. The fly agaric mushroom doesn't produce nearly as pleasant of an experience as the popular psilocybe. On the contrary, it produces painful reactions such as delirium, vomiting, dizziness, drooling, twitching, and sweating.

Can the Magic Mushroom Be Addictive?

While there is little evidence to support an addiction to magic mushrooms, it is possible to develop tolerance and require a greater and more frequent doses due to regular use. Experienced users indulge in the experience only occasionally and approach it with great appreciation and mindfulness. The main benefit of consuming these mushrooms consists of gaining profound personal insights and then applying them to benefit your life and those you love.

If you resort to over-using the mushrooms to induce artificial pleasant experiences, these experiences will have only a superficial meaning, and you will start to crave more over time. As you start to consume the mushrooms increasingly, your tolerance will increase as well. This puts you at a higher risk of taking large doses, which can result in symptoms similar to an overdose. Although these symptoms aren't life-threatening, they can be profoundly difficult and disturbing. Having a "bad trip" or experience filled with dreadful hallucinations and paranoia can be followed by a prolonged sense of panic, which can then lead to psychosis and seizures. When it comes to the physical symptoms, the overuse of mushrooms can lead to weakness in your muscles, diarrhea, vomiting, and agitation. It is also possible that these symptoms persist long after the effects of the psychedelic have subsided. While the effect of the mushrooms lasts only up to six hours, after which it will be eliminated from your system, the long-term personality changes can be both positive and negative.

The use of this psychedelic comes with both advantages and possible risks. Responsibility and accountability for your safety and well-being is particularly important, as the consumption of this mushroom can lead to long-term positive personality changes, but also long-term negative changes that will be hard to overcome if you choose the wrong type of mushrooms or mismatch the dosage with your needs and personal capacity to process the chemical and the experiences.

Emotional Effects

Psilocybin affects numerous brain structures, as it serves to modulate serotonergenic neurotransmission. Essentially, psilocybin stimulates the neurological process normally induced by serotonin, mimicking its effect in a way. Normally, your brain would excrete serotonin while you're exercising, having fun, or sharing intimate moments. However, the psychoactive compound has the ability to produce the same chemical effect without the necessity of any particular activity. This shows the therapeutic potential of the substance. However, the most important impact of the substance reflects in its effect on emotional face processing, which is mainly involved with different affective disorders and anxiety.

Psilocybin and Emotional Processing

To better understand the emotional impact of psilocybin, it's important to also understand how the process of emotional processing works. Your amygdala, a small part located in the center of the brain that is most often associated with fear processing, is also in charge of processing anger, anxiety, and other negative emotions. However, this part of the brain, when overactive, creates a bias against positive emotions, which means that it enhances negative responses to positive stimuli to induce negative responses. An unbalanced amygdala can impair emotional processing, which means that it can worsen depression and anxiety. This state can make you perceive only the negatives and overlook any positive sides of a situation or experience. This creates a negative mindset, albeit with an added bonus of training your brain to further intensify the negative tendency due to self-imposed isolation and unhealthy lifestyle, ever-present in anxiety and depression. Psilocybin, in fact, shows the potential to help stop and reprogram these neurophysiological patterns and rewire your brain for positivity.

Some studies showed that psilocybin can help restore balance in the parts of the brain in charge of emotional processing, inducing similar effects to antidepressants. The antidepressant effects of psilocybin reflect in its impact on the limbic system and the prefrontal cortex of the brain, which also includes the fear-inducing amygdala. Psilocybin also links to restoring balance in connections between frontal pole nodes, which is also associated with emotional processing. Overall, the main argument for the use of psilocybin in medicinal purposes is that it gives the brain a chance to start processing feelings in a more balanced, rational way. While 'rational' might be the last word you'd use when discussing psychoactive mushrooms, it is the effect that they produce when introduced into a mind that's wired for irrational negativity.

The Amygdala-Modulant That Balances Feelings

To better understand how the magic mushrooms can help you restore emotional balance, it's important to understand how their chemical compounds affect the amygdala. Psilocybin is a major modulator of the amygdala's connectivity hubs. Studies that examined how this compound affects emotions face discrimination. It was found that this occurrence decreases during happy times, reduced fearful and angry physiological responses. These studies confirmed the modulatory effect of psilocybin. The results showed that psilocybin acted as a modulator of the amygdala's connectivity hubs, which means that it altered the ways this part of the brain reacts in response to anger and fear. It was shown that the responses in the amygdala decreased when it was experiencing anger and fear.

Simply put, psilocybin showed the potential to reduce one's emotional response to negative feelings, which can be viewed as supportive of emotional stability.

However, studies have yet to show whether or not this hallucinogen has the potential to be used for therapeutic purposes with certainty of positive outcomes and the elimination of negative outcomes.

The "Happy Chemical"

Due to previously described effects, psilocybin has earned a reputation for being a happiness-inducing chemical. But, how does this effect occur? Psilocybin affects the same neural pathways that are impacted by serotonin, which is yet another happiness hormone. Technically, the potent chemical derived from the mushroom stimulates these neural pathways, helping emotional and mood regulation. It affects the similar areas of the brain that are activated with the impact of serotonin, leading to hallucinations as it decreases the functioning of the thalamus. As a result, your mood improves and there's a greater possibility of decreasing the side effects of depression.

What one can conclude is that the use of magic mushrooms can increase the sense of happiness, at least temporarily, and reduce fear. This is an important piece of information as it suggests that the mushroom may, indeed, be used to alleviate symptoms of anxiety and depression. However, it is important to note that the effect of psilocybin isn't isolated. This means that one shouldn't use it for therapeutic purposes without caution. Mushrooms contain other psychoactive substances as well, and if combined with traditional medication, like antidepressants, can create emotional effects of unpredictable nature and uncertain intensity.

Sensory effects

Psilocybin, the most potent chemical inside the mushroom, is a fungal alkaloid that appears naturally. It is present in over 100 mushroom species. Once consumed, the chemical will then break down inside the stomach and create psilocin, which is the basic component of the effect that these mushrooms create. After that, it will create the effects that alter the state of mind.

While there's little risk associated with the use of mushrooms, it is possible that taking high doses can result in unpleasant effects. The risks include a wide range of sensory reactions that can impair your judgment and create a feeling of isolation. It is also known to induce panic attacks or a negative hallucination experience, also known as 'bad trip.' The substances found in psilocybin mushrooms can also create flashbacks that can be persistent and recurring. These flashbacks can significantly impair functioning in the period before the effect of the drug subsides. However, the condition can worsen to develop a hallucinogen persisting perceptual disorder (HPDD). If this state lasts through prolonged periods of time, it can intervene with normal daily functioning.

Sensory effects of psilocybin can cause psychosis when the drug is taken persistently and in high dosage. The symptoms of this disorder include paranoia, mood swings, disorganized state of mind, problems with vision, and others.

Short-Term Effects

However, the short-term effects of the mushroom depend on the amount consumed and the frequency of consumption, as well as the type of mushroom. Intense sensory and emotional experiences, mental regression to past experiences, perceived spiritual experiences, visual hallucinations, and other sensory effects are present after the use of the mushroom.

One of the more interesting effects that the mushroom can produce is the state called synesthesia, which blends different sensations. This effect can cause you to see sound, taste or hear colors.

However, there are many potentially dangerous sensory effects of the mushroom, like high risk of accidents due to altered vision, hearing, impaired judgment, and time perception. The hallucinogens can alter the state of mind to produce completely distorted thinking, exposing you to the risk of deadly accidents.

With the potential to induce paranoia, intense mood swings, or disorganized thoughts, this naturally-occurring hallucinogen can also cause suicidal tendencies or aggressive behavior.

However, not all sensory effects of the mushroom are this severe. Most often, it generates a feeling of relaxation and weakness in muscles. Problems with coordinating your eyes can also occur as well as intense sweating and increased blood pressure. Breathing and heart rate irregularity is common as a side effect of use, which can but doesn't have to, increase the sense of paranoia or the perceived risk of a panic attack. Dilated pupils are most commonly present after use.

Usually, psilocybin mushrooms induce an effect that persists for about 20 minutes after use. However, it is possible that the effect lasts up to a couple of hours. In fact, the effects of the mushroom can persist up to six hours after use. On most occasions, users feel only mild relaxation. However, the effect increases with the dosage which means that it's possible that taking a higher dose would result in stronger side effects or negative outcomes, such as paranoia or negative hallucinations. What's important to note is that the intensity of the reaction increases after each use, meaning that the initial effects will be weaker and increase until they reach a peak, after which they'll start to decline in intensity.

Long-Term Use

Long-term consumption of psilocybin increases the chances of negative side effects, such as drug-induced psychosis. This is a state in which one's thoughts are disorganized, and the ability to communicate with others is impaired. This psychosis can persist after the acute period. There's also the presence of paranoia, which can create a profoundly negative experience, paired with visual hallucinations and problems as well as severe mood swings.

As mentioned earlier, these psychoactive substances can also cause severe, persistent flashbacks that may result in sensory distortions. While flashbacks, on their own, are difficult to experience, they can also persist long after you stop using the drug. In fact, they can persist for years.

While there's a relatively low risk of developing an addiction to psilocybin, there is a risk of problematic use that can lead to negative health outcomes. There's the possibility of developing a hallucinogen use disorder, which becomes a pattern of dysfunctional use whenever one encounters distress or emotionally challenging circumstances.

This can happen if you take larger amounts than you intended or fail to quit using it. If the time that takes to recover from the effect of hallucinogen starts to increase, especially if followed by the increased urges for consuming these mushrooms, this compound can impair the capacity of working or learning. This can intervene with one's normal daily life, work, and education. It can also cause irresponsible and neglectful behaviors without any success in quitting.

This can also cause the impairment or reduction of healthy daily activities, like in your social groups and professional groups, and lead to safety risks when driving. Sadly, the syndrome may cause one to persist with using psilocybin despite the negative side effects. Simultaneously, the amount of the drug needed to induce the symptoms increases.

To quit using these mushrooms after excessive use, it's less likely that a classic drug addiction approach will be needed. Instead, it is recommended to use emotional coping skills and correct one's negative behavioral patterns, along with the examination and questioning of the belief system. If quitting proves too difficult for an individual, the help of medication and therapists can be invaluable in surpassing the habit of using it continuously.

Dosage

The effects of magic mushrooms can vary depending on the dosage. To increase the chances of positive effects and reduce the risks of negative effects, it is important to understand how to dose the mushroom properly. The proper dosage mainly depends on the type of mushroom but also on how it is being consumed. You will consume different amounts if the mushroom is dried than if it is cooked, and you'll use different dosages if the therapeutic substance is prepared in the form of tea.

It is important to develop a responsible approach to taking these psychedelics, especially if you're a beginner. With the proper dosage, the magic mushroom can create pleasant experiences and help you reduce stress, balance your mood, and feel overall happier.

Before we begin discussing the dosage of psilocybin mushrooms, it is important to remind you to check the legality of using them in your environment, because it is your responsibility for purchasing and consuming these mushrooms . With the proper use and dosage, you will consume the substance safely and reap the benefits without experiencing mental imbalance associated with excessive use. However, it is important to note that feeling the increased urge to consume these mushrooms may be a sign of developing a dysfunctional relationship with them for which the assistance of therapists and medical experts will be urgent and important to avoid long-term impairment of cognitive and emotional balance.

The use and dosage of psilocybin mushrooms depend on the purpose you're using it for. A light dosage of the drug will induce a feeling of happiness and interesting visual experiences.

Microdosing

Microdosing of the mushrooms limits you to consuming 0.2–0.5 grams of dried mushrooms. However, if you're using fresh mushrooms, you may take between two and five grams. If this is your first time using recreational substances, you should stick to the lower end of the scale to prevent any negative effects. Microdosing doesn't cause impairment of judgment, loss of control, visual changes or disturbances; it merely boosts your energy and creativity. With a minimal dose, you will be able to observe the experience with a clear mind and decide whether you want to proceed with more intensity or stick to the lowest dosage for an occasional boost of creativity and profound relaxation.

Moderate a.k.a "Happy" Dose

If you take between half and a single gram of the dried mushrooms, you'll feel like you're floating in the clouds. This is a more intense effect that may intervene with your daily activities, which is why it's recommended to use this dosage only when you're in a safe, trusted environment, like a friendly gathering, or during the weekend, when you're at home with someone you trust and love.

Chapter 5 Different Types Of Magic Mushrooms

In many countries all over the world, psilocybin-containing mushrooms are available. Archeological investigations sometimes find examples of magic mushrooms or connections to them. Commentators such as the late Terence McKenna indicated that early hominids who consumed magic mushrooms were inspired to create a sophisticated language and religion, contributing to more complex cultures.

There is no doubt that psilocybin is a great drug, but if you collect wild mushrooms, please be careful.

Right identification is critical in general when working with the fungi. A few poisonous animals mimic a variety of magic mushrooms. Adverse reactions will range from mild diarrhea to anaphylaxis and sometimes even death. Please be 100% certain before ingesting food that has not been produced from known spores. At maximum, heading into the forest is reckless and, at worst, suicide, picking up those mystery shrooms and swallowing them. The mushroom you want to kill is going to have specific conditions it thrives under. The important factors are temperature, humidity, medium development, and the time of year. It's also essential to know your target's life cycle. Based on parent mycelium, the fruiting body usually only exists for a few months or every few years.

There are thousands of mushroom species in the world, but because of their hallucinogenic properties, Psilocybin Mushrooms have become more common. Yet did you know that there are other kinds of magic mushrooms that can also cause psychedelic effects? This book lists the various types of hallucinogenic mushrooms, their sources, their symptoms, and their characteristics.

Here are the most common psilocybin mushrooms.

Psilocybe Mushrooms

Psilocybe is a type of mushroom best known for its psychoactive compounds: psilocybin, psilocybin, and biocytin.

Typically small are the fruit bodies of the mushrooms that belong to this group, distinguished by their small to medium caps, brown to yellow coloration, and a spore-print varying from lilac brown to dark purple-gray. Likewise, this sort of magic mushrooms appears to bruise when treated. All organisms belonging to this group grow on the organic matter, which is rotting. Psychedelic effects occur 20-60 minutes after Psilocybe cubensis has been swallowed, and these results can last from 4-10 hours. Such results include optical distortion, vivid color enhancement, and realistic forms of animation. 20-60 minutes after Psilocybe cubensis is swallowed, symptoms that can last from 4-10 hours can be anticipated. Such results include optical illusions, vivid color enhancement, and organically formed animation.

Two common organisms of the genus Psilocybe are:

Psilocybin Cubensis. Possibly the most common of all Psilocybes, this species is also known as shrooms or cubes. The diversity is rising throughout the globe. In the United States Gulf Coast, Brazil, Central America, South America, West Indies, Vietnam, Indonesia, Asia, and Australia, it rises on cow dung. Thanks to their conic to convex caps, which can expand from 2 and 8 cm in diameter anywhere, they can be easily identified. Their reddish-cinnamon colored color transforms with age to a golden brown, which also contributed to their street name, gold hats. This includes psilocybin, biocytin, and psilocin. The concentrations of each material in this species differ, owing to factors such as age.

Psilocybe Cyanescens. This form is also known as wavy caps because of their tops, which, when maturing, are clearly wavy. Because of its light buff and yellowish color, the caps are quite distinctive within its class. These also have very characteristic blackish-brown spores. In the US, P. cyanescens spreads south of the San Francisco Bay area in the Pacific Northwest. Throughout Western and Central Africa, Canada, Western Asia, Western Europe, Central Europe, and New Zealand, it also develops. They develop along the perimeters of urban areas and mulched beds on woodchips. Because of the fruiting needs of this species, it is difficult to grow them indoors.

Psilocybe Semilanceata. This fungus grows in grasslands, and especially in wetlands. In comparison to P. cubensis, it does not develop on dung. It feeds on diminishing grassroots and is distributed in 17 northern hemisphere countries, especially in North America, Canada, Russia, Switzerland, Poland, and the Netherlands.

Often known as the caps of liberty are semilanceata. Their caps range in form from distinctly conical to bell-shaped, with a pronounced tip that looks like a breast.

Psilocybe Azurescens. This is the most active psilocybin-containing mushrooms at 1.78 percent psilocybin amounts. People new to magic mushrooms should, for the first time, avoid eating more than an 8th of P. azurescens. The animal is incredibly robust and twice as effective as the P. cubensis.

The cap has a diameter of 30-100 mm and flattened with age. They are found along a small area of the West Coast of the United States, among coastal dune grasses. A handful of endangered species are also in Germany.

Conocybe Mushrooms

Some forms of monocyte mushrooms have long, thin, delicate stems, which thrive on dead vegetation, dead turf, sand dunes, decayed trees, and dung in rich grasslands. Thanks to their conical or bell-shaped caps, Conocybe members are called coneheads. The genus monocyte contains at least 243 varieties of mushrooms, four of which contain psilocin and psilocybin, the hallucinogenic compounds.

Conocybe kehneriana. Not much of this fungus is established, but it occurs in Norway and Argentina. Its physical appearance is similar to that of those belonging to the genus Conocybe.

Conocybe siligineoids. This fungus is also known as cone caps and is thin, low, and only around 3 inches in height. The hat is reddish-orange with a bell-shaped color. This gets a rusty color as spores develop. In other parts of the world, it is hardly ever seen. Both collections have been obtained in Mexico, where they were originally reported to be a medicinal mushroom used in curing and numerous ceremonies. They are either fresh or in the form of tea, drunk by locals.

Conocybe cyanopus/Pholiotina cyanopus. Currently, this fungus is allocated to the genus Pholiotina but was referred to the genus Conocybe in 1935. It is a tiny mushroom with a conic to narrowly convex cap that develops on decaying matter and is smooth and colored cinnamon brown. It is relatively small, with stripped margins typically less than 25 mm wide. The base is flat and delicate at the bottom with whitish areas, and the rest is brownish. The spores are gray with cinnamon as well. Because of its strong resemblance to toxic plants, most mycologists warn against gathering and consuming this plant. Another feature of this species is its Sclerotia capacitance, a sleeping shape that in the fruiting body grows underground. Sclerotia are commonly called truffles. In the temperate regions of North America,

Australia, Belgium, Denmark, Finland, France, Germany, Hungary, Latvia, the Netherlands, Norway, Poland, Russia, Sweden, Canada, Ukraine, and the United States, this plant occurs throughout lawns, parks and grassy areas.

Conocybe smithii/Pholiotina smithii. Compared to the previous group, it is now reclassified into the genus Pholiotina. P. smithii is found in North America in moors, ditches, and sumptuous fields of sphagnum moose. It is located around the banks of the river and on lawns, too. It is known to occur in northern Michigan, in Alberta, California, Wisconsin, Idaho, and on historic man-made earthen mounds. This bears fruit in the early summer.

The caps of the smithii measure 0.3-1 cm across with a conic to convex form that grows to almost smooth with age. The cinnamon-brown color matches the color of its spores.

Thanks to their resemblance to poisonous mushrooms, authorities warn firmly against the use of them in psychedelic studies, given their slight hallucinogenic effects.

Copelandia/Panaeolus Mushrooms

Copelandia is a genus consisting of 12 varieties of mushrooms, all known to contain the psilocin and psilocybin hallucinogens. American and European mycologists also decided to list within Panaeolus all members of the genus Copelandia.

Mushrooms of the genus Panaeolus are white to gray or brown, with large, thin, delicate stalks. These are distributed throughout both hemisphere's tropics and neotropics, emerging in grasslands, dry vegetation, dying grass, sand dunes, decayed trees, and dung. They continue to bruise and turn blue owing to their psilocin material.

Representative organisms within the genus Panaeolus are:

- **Panaeolus cambodginiensis.** This is a potent hallucinogenic mushroom with psilocybin and psilocin in it. The convex-shaped hat is less than 23 mm long. The color of the cap is flat, with gills gray to black. This is in line with its black spores, too. It developed on water buffalo dung and was first seen in Cambodia but has proven to be a common occurrence across the subtropics of Asia and Hawaii.

- **Panaeolus cyanescens.** This is another psilocybin mushroom of the group mentioned above. The tip, when small, is 1.5-4 cm across with an incurved edge. The color is yellow or brownish, but when impaired, it turns green or blue. The spores are black plane. It is also a habitat populated by dung that frequents pastures in Europe, India, areas of Asia, North America, and South America.

- **Panaeolus bisporus.** This specimen visually looks no different from the P. cambodginiensis. It can be identified just under a microscope. The thin brawn fungus grows in dung and has black spores. We are located in Hawaii, southern California, North Africa, Switzerland, and Spain.

- **Panaeolus tropicalis.** This is one of the most active psilocybin mushrooms under the family Copelandia / Panaeolus. The cap is 1,5-2,5 cm wide, clay-colored, and is hemispheric to convex. The stem is about 5-12 cm long, becoming blackish towards the middle. When it is scratched, it turns blue.

Tropical often grows on dung and is most frequently found in Hawaii, Cambodia, and Central Africa. Growing can also be seen in China, Uganda, the Philippines, Florida, and Japan.

Galerina Mushrooms

Galerina is a category of tiny, brown-spored mushrooms that grow on decaying matter with more than 300 species worldwide–from the far north to the isolated Southern Ocean Macquarie Island. Species that belong to this group are typically small with a short, delicate base. They are growing in mossy and forest environments.

Of the many mushroom species under the genus Galerina, only one is known to produce psilocybin. Most species below this group are toxic indeed.

ü **Galerina steglichii.** This amongst the forms of magic mushrooms is extremely rare. In Germany, they're mentioned only once. We expand in singular numbers or in few.

Such mushrooms can be described by their 2-3 mm diameter brown caps. The spores make the orange-brown prints dirty.

Inocybe Mushrooms

Inocybe is a genus of fungi that form mushrooms. Inocybe members live inside the roots of vascular host plants. Because of this, mushroom types are amongst the most highly adaptable.

Under this genus, typical mushrooms are brown, although some species are lilac. Their caps are usually tiny and conical, though they flatten with age. Some caps, defined as spermatic or musty, have a distinctive odor.

4 Species are known to produce psychedelic effects under this genus.

ü **Inocybe aeruginascens.** The first specimen was reported on 15 June 1965. They are also widely distributed in temperate areas and have been recorded in damp, sandy soils in central Europe and western North America. Such mushrooms are tiny with a conical to convex cap that typically has a diameter of less than 5 cm. The color of the cap ranges from buff to light yellow-gray, typically with greenish stains that fade when the mushrooms dry. The spores are flat, and they create a brown clay print. These include psychoactive substances such as psilocybin, psilocin, biocytin, and a newly found substance called aeruginascin. I, so far. The only form of magic mushroom that creates aeruginascin is aeruginescens.

ü **Inocybe coelestium.** That type of magic mushroom is widely distributed in Europe. The name "coelestium" indicates the people of Mount Olympus, the "celestials." This is a reference to its hallucinogenic qualities. The physical properties are generally similar to most members of the genus Inocybe.

ü **Inocybe haematite.** This species has a strong similarity to the I. Aeruginescensicens. This mystical fungus is rising in European coastal areas.

ü **Inocybe tricolor.** The Inocybe member group is found in temperate forests. It also includes psilocybin, as well as psilocin. It's found in central Europe, in Norway. The hat is brick red to dark sugar, deeper to the fringes. It is normally 4 cm in diameter and contains spores that are ochre or tan gray.

Mycena Mushrooms

This broad genus consists of mushrooms which develop on decaying matter as well. Rarely more than a few centimeters long, they sport a white spore print, a narrow bell-shaped tip, and a short, delicate base. Most of the mushrooms are gray or brown under the genus Mycena.

These are hard to distinguish from other types of mushrooms and need to be viewed to identify under a microscope. Some species are toxic, while others are toxin-free. One of these contains the psilocybin hallucinogen.

ü **Mycena cyanorrhiza.** This is a green, tiny mushroom with a blue shell. It is seen emerging in wood forests and leaves a white print on the spore.

Psilocybin is stated to contain, but this is probably a false statement. The edibility is uncertain, and it has no historical record of being used as a hallucinogen.

ü **Pluteus mushrooms.** This group includes over 300 organisms that grow on wood or wood remains. We drop pink spore prints and gills that are separate from the stem. Some of these mushrooms are edible though most people rate their flavor and quality as average. Many representatives of this group bruise blue when treated, a warning that they produce psilocybin.

ü **Pluteus brunneidiscus.** Brunneidiscus is first found in Spain and the United States as an agaric fungus genus. Between June to November, it develops solitary on the forests of trees with large leaves.

ü **Pluteus salacious.** The mystical German fungus spreads on wood. The silver-gray caps which span 2-8 cm in diameter can be recognized. It also has tiny scales near the center, brighter at the top, and when wet, becomes somewhat translucent. The stem measures 3-5 cm long at the root and is slightly swollen. Psilocybin and psilocin concentrations in dried P. salacious samples are recorded within the range of 0.21-0.35 percent and 0.011 and 0.05 percent, respectively.

Chapter 6 How To Find And Recognize A Psilocybin Mushrooms

Knowing how to identify wild mushrooms is a great skill set to have. It allows you to go out and forage for some of the food that you eat while getting in touch with nature. Wild mushrooms are delicacies and while it would be wonderful if we could purchase them at the store, as of right now, it just is not an option. This means that if you want these amazing treats on your plate, you are going to have to learn how to identify them.

There are many reasons that a person may want to learn how to identify mushrooms. One of the main reasons is because they want to eat them. Mushrooms come in a variety of flavors and with some great aromas.

Searching for mushrooms can be very fulfilling as well. It gives us an opportunity to connect with the Earth while getting away from the hustle and bustle that we have to deal with every day. You can't rush around looking for mushrooms. You have to be patient in order to find them.

Mushroom hunting is a great way to get outside and get some extra exercise. Taking the family along will give you the opportunity to teach them a new skill and it will provide them with the chance to relax as well.

The health benefits of wild mushrooms are amazing as well. Wild mushrooms have been proven to provide you with a huge energy boost and they can boost your immune system as well. The wild mushrooms are free as well which makes them that much better.

Imagine that you are walking through the woods after a beautiful late spring rain. It is warm outside but not too warm. The Earth smells clean. Suddenly you step on a pile of leaves and your feet fly out from under you. As you open your eyes you find yourself lying on the ground looking at the most delicious looking mushrooms you have ever laid your eyes on. Are they though? In order to know if the mushrooms are something that you are going to be able to eat or something that is going to put you in the hospital, you have to start by learning how to identify the parts of the mushroom.

As we already stated, the mushroom is just the fruit and it is part of an entire root system that could be huge.

As you can see in this picture, the cap is the very top part of the mushroom. It looks like a little open umbrella. You will want to pay very close attention to the caps of the mushrooms.

On the underside of the cap is where you will find the gills. These are also a very important part of identifying edible mushrooms.

The stalk is the stem on which the cap sits, and the mycelium is the system of roots found beneath the forest floor.

It is very important to understand the different mushroom parts when you are learning how to identify mushrooms because you want to be able to understand exactly what it is that you are looking for. In order to identify wild mushrooms, we have to be aware of as well as understand their parts. This is because many of them have poisonous look a likes. If you were to just look at a picture of these mushrooms you would risk grabbing the poisonous one. However, when you learn about their parts you are increasing the chances of you getting the mushroom that you want to find.

I want to start with the easiest mushrooms to identify. These mushrooms are known as the foolproof four. These are the best species for you to start looking for because they are edible and very easy to identify.

Chanterelle

The Chanterelle mushroom is a beautiful mushroom that resembles a flower and is known as a delicacy. The flesh can be orange to yellow and the mushrooms have a fruity smell.

The cap is usually yellow to orange with wavy or curled edges. Some of the edges can be curled up and some will be curled down. A younger chanterelle will have more of a flat top.

The gills under the cap of the mushroom are going to be very thick and narrow. The veins will be interconnected. The stalk will be a light orange or a pale yellow color that tapers at the bottom.

The spores of these mushrooms are going to be yellow. The mushrooms can be medium in size to large when they are fully grown. You will find these in the fall all the way up to early spring. These are usually found in the woods or forests, often right under trees. You can find these mushrooms all over the western US and all the way into Alaska.

Morel

Morel mushrooms are one of the most prized of all edible mushrooms. They have what people describe as a honeycomb cap, or brain like cap. They have an amazing rich flavor that people fall in love with over and over again.

The cap of the Morel is going to be round or oval in shape. It often resembles a brain or honeycomb. You will find that it is light brown to brown in color and has darker holes throughout the cap. You will not be able to see any gills on this mushroom. The stalk is often lighter than the cap, a very light brown to white color. You will not see spores because of the lack of gills.

The morel mushroom can grow from 1 inch all the way up to 12 inches tall. I have seen them so large that they had to be sliced into "steaks" in order to be cooked.

You will find the morels in the spring, in an area that is located near a stream or river because of the sandy soils. They grow in dark wet places usually where leaves litter the ground. The best time to find morel mushrooms is right after a spring rain when the sun pops out.

Morel mushrooms can be found all across North America.

Western Giant Puffball

The Western Giant Puffball looks like a great big snowball or a balloon. It is round or can be oblong. You should pick them when the flesh is firm and white all the way through. You do not want to eat them when the flesh is green or yellow because it does cause stomach upset. You will find that when the mushroom is young, the flesh is white. When they have reached maturity, the flesh will be brown or a greenish brown color.

The cap of the western giant puffball is going to be white or white with light brown markings all over. You will not be able to see the gills and there is no stalk. Spores are located around the sacks. A western giant puffball can grow as large as 10 inches in diameter and you can find them growing in the summer to the fall. You will find the western giant puffball in areas such as grassy fields, lawns, near rotting wood, on hillsides or near the road. You can find them all over North America.

Hen Of the Woods Or Sulfur Shelf

This is another very beautiful mushroom that many people think tastes like chicken. The flesh of the mushroom can be yellow to orange and it looks like shelves as it grows on the side of trees.

The cap of this mushroom is going to be yellow to orange with an edge that is brighter in color than the rest of the mushroom. The older the mushroom the lighter in color they are. You will find that older hen of the woods are hardened and woody in flavor. The younger ones will be damp and rubbery.

The gills are located on the underside and are bright yellow pores. The stalk is going to be extremely short and stubby. It may look as if there is no stalk because it is connected to the bark of the tree. The spores from this mushroom will be white.

The hen of the woods can be as small as 2 inches to 20 inches long on a tree. You will find these from mid-summer into fall. You will find them growing on the wood of trees such as cherry, chestnut, beech, willow, and oak. They usually start at the base of the tree and grow up.

These are found all across North America.

Spore Prints

To add to all of the information that you have learned this far about identifying mushrooms, I want to take a moment and talk about spore prints. As you have read about the last four mushrooms you may have noticed that I talked about their spores, where they were located, and even the color of them. Why? Because spore prints can help you learn a lot about the mushrooms that you are collecting. Take one of the caps that you have collected, making sure that the stem is removed and put it on a piece of paper. Place a jar upside down on top of the mushroom in order to ensure that no air gets in.

Come back the next day and carefully remove the jar. Lift up the cap and you are going to find spores on your sheet of paper. These spores should match the spores that we have talked about. For example, if I tell you that the spores are going to be white and you find black spores, you know you have picked the wrong mushroom.

Using spore prints to identify your mushrooms is going to ensure that you do not make any mistakes. If your spore prints match and you have used all of the other information given to you to identify the mushroom, chances are, you have got the right one. Its also a great way to learn more about the mushrooms that you are picking. There are literally tens of thousands of different types of mushrooms out there that you can eat. While I am going to try to cover as many as I can throughout this book, I can only cover so many. So, let's get into some more mushrooms

Boletes

The boletes is known as a porcini mushroom or belonging to a large species of mushrooms that contain lots of edible species of mushrooms but not a single deadly one. This does not mean that they are all okay for you to eat. If you eat some of them, you may end up wishing that you were dead because of the amount of pain that you will be in.

However, the bolete is edible and very enjoyable. There are a few things that you need to know about the bolete to ensure that you are picking the right mushroom.

As you can see in the picture the cap of the bolete is very dense and there are no gills underneath. Instead of gills, the bolete is going to have pores under the cap which will release the spores. The pores look much different from the gills on other mushrooms. It is spongy.

Coral Fungi

These mushrooms as you may have already guessed by their name resemble coral. They have also been said to resemble clubs and antlers. They come in a variety of colors and are edible. The tubular branches have a smooth appearance and are topped with a small crown. The stalks have a firm texture even though this mushroom is very fragile. They are tender and very delicate.

You will usually find this mushroom near decaying logs from summer to fall. It is very important for you to use extreme caution when you are hunting for the coral fungi because there are species that look similar that are incredibly toxic. Make sure that you avoid any mushroom that is brightly colored. You should only eat the beige, white, or yellow coral fungi.

You can eat these mushrooms raw, but they will usually upset the stomach. Instead, try battering them and frying them up as appetizers.

Fairy Ring Mushroom

The fairy ring mushroom is one that grows all across North America and can be found in fields, lawns, and dunes. They tend to grow where a stump used to be. You can find the fairy ring mushrooms in the summer and fall months. These can be found all year long in warmer climates.

These mushrooms grow in a ring or sometimes an arc. The caps can be anywhere from 1 to 5 centimeters wide. When the mushroom is young the cap may be rolled downward. However, as they get older you will find that the edges become turned up. The mushroom is dry, and it is bald as well. They are usually a pale tan or brown but can be white as well. The stem is extremely tough and is one of the ways that many people identify this mushroom. The mushroom does have gills and the spores will be white. There is a dangerous look alike. It looks very similar to the fairy ring mushroom; however, the stem is not as strong. You will also notice that the gills are very crowded when compared to the gills of a fairy ring.

Field Mushroom

You can find the field mushroom all over North America, in Europe, Asia, New Zealand, and in Africa. They are generally found in grassy places and can grown near the fairy ring or they can grow on their own.

The field mushroom is going to have a white cap that is up to 10 centimeters in diameter. The cap is usually flat when the mushroom has matured. Under the cap there are gills that are pink in the younger mushrooms. The gills turn reddish-brown as the mushroom grows and then turn complete dark brown as the mushroom reaches maturity. The stalk of the field mushroom can be up to 10 centimeters tall. The flesh will bruise reddish-brown and the spores are dark brown.

You should get rid of any mushroom that you think is a field mushroom if the gills are not pink. You have to be very careful when you are picking this type of mushroom because the look alike is fatal. The Amanita virosa looks much like the field mushroom, however, just one cap of amanita virosa can kill a person. The gills are white, and the spores are white as well. These are the destroying angel mushrooms. They are one of the most dangerous mushrooms out there.

There are other look a likes as well which can cause a serious upset stomach. The agaricus xanthodermus can be identified by the yellow stain that will appear when you cut the stem. This is why it is so important for you to make sure that you are picking the right mushroom.

Shaggy Inkcap

The shaggy ink cap is found across North America as well as in Europe in meadows and grasslands. You will be able to find this mushroom between June and November depending on how hot it is. It is important to know that this mushroom is only edible when it is young, before the gills have become black. The shaggy ink cap is going to have a cap that will droop over the majority of the stem when it is young, and it looks as if it is covered in scales.

You have to be quick in order to harvest this mushroom because the gills will turn from white to pink and then black very quickly. You cannot eat this mushroom once the gills turn black.

There is a dangerous look alike that is often confused with the shaggy ink cap which is called the maned agaric. This mushroom can cause diarrhea, vomiting and many other unpleasant symptoms especially if eaten after consuming alcohol. While these symptoms can be very scary, they will go away as long as you do not consume more alcohol. The severity of the symptoms caused by this mushroom are going to depend on the amount of alcohol that you have consumed. If you have not consumed any alcohol, it is not likely that this mushroom will make you very ill.

Lions Mane Mushroom

You can find this mushroom all over the world. It is easily found in forests though. This mushroom like many others that we have talked about will usually grow in a well shaded area, near or on a rotten log.

You are most likely to find this mushroom in the autumn months. It looks like a bunch of little icicles dangling from the log. All of the white parts of this mushroom are edible. The great thing about this mushroom is that there are no look a likes in North America. You can eat all four of the species found there. It is possible that in some remote part of the world there is a dangerous look a like though.

Black Trumpet

The black trumpet can be found all across North America and is most likely to be found near oak or beech trees. You will find this mushroom near streams or rivers because they prefer the dark damp area.

You can find this mushroom during the summer and the fall; in the southern areas of North America you may be able to find it through the winter.

These mushrooms can be difficult to find because they grow in leaf litter. If you do find one though you are very lucky because they grow in clusters. The cap is going to be a very dark black, brown or a grey color. It is going to be shaped like a trumpet or a vase. The underside of the cap is smooth, you will not find any pores, gills, or teeth. You may find that the cap has some small scales but most of the cap should be smooth or have just a few wrinkles.

Chapter 7 How To Grow Magic Mushrooms At Home

The Growing Process Step By Step

Step 1: The starting point is to prepare the room to grow and make sure it has no dust or mould problems.

Step 2: The next step is to configure the Bunsen burner and make sure it is stable; in no case can it fall to the side!

Step 3: Hit the Psilocybin mushroom spores, needles and Petri dishes. For now, keep the nuts in the Petri dishes, and they should only be opened when needed and closed immediately after completion.

Step 4: position printing Spore Psilocybin mushrooms over on the table, keep the front of the needle in the flame of the Bunsen burner and keep it up to when start making some red. Then let it cool. Keep it back in the flame for about 3-5 seconds. Wait a few seconds and make sure that no more than room temperature in the press releases the spores, open Petri dishes and place the back end of the needle in the agar and close to the Petri dish. Remember that everything must be done very quickly and that the Petri dish cannot be opened for more than 3 seconds, and it is better not to completely remove the lid, lift it and move it to leave only 1 or 2 cm of space directly exposed to the air.

Step 5: make sure it is made with 3 Petri dishes and put them in a dark room at medium temperature. Avoid exposing them to direct sunlight, as it could be negative and negatively heat Petri dishes. Humidity will not be a problem, because the Petri dish is a beautiful small breeding chamber. In 4-10 days, you will see how the Psilocybin mushroom started to colonize through the agar-agar.

Step 6: If your Psilocybin mushroom spores have already been colonized in a petri dish, they are prepared for the next step. Prepare a mixture of 1 part of rice flour and 1 part of vermiculite and three parts of organic rye. Distribute the mixture in an amount that perfectly fits your bottles. Even if you're sure it's sterile after this step, try to avoid unnecessary dust, dirt or harmful environments, such as moldy rooms. Before placing the lid, add 2 cups of coffee to each jar.

Step 7: place the canned jars in the pressure cooker, seal and cook over low heat. Since the storage jars are made of glass, they can break if they overheat and cool too quickly. When the pressure cooker is completely hot, leave it for 60 minutes. The steam is not as hot as the Bunsen burner, so they need more time for sterilization.

Step 8: when the bottles are sterile, let them cool down to room temperature, but they should never go wrong when opening the bottle lid, otherwise it would run the risk of contamination.

Step 9: take a scalpel and Petri dishes, which are now colonized with hallucinogenic mushrooms. Sterilize the scalpel on the top of the Bunsen burner and allow it to cool, open the lid of the Petri dishes and carefully cut the colonized agar into squares to obtain about 5-10 small colonized pieces.

Step 10: wear sterile gloves and, if possible, wear long tweezers also sterile. Open the lid, take the jars and push the colonized agar pieces and close them. Do it the same way you put the hallucinogenic fungal spores on the Petri dishes.

Step 11: Keep balloons in the darkroom with an average temperature, as in the case of capsules of Petri, after a few days, you will realize that the colonization of Psilocybin mushrooms digs their power agents. Remember that passage moving on to the next stage, which is very important for colonizing until it fills half the bottle.

Step 12: prepare the same mixture of the soil of crop that has been placed in cans and adds the same amount of water by placing them in a pressure cooker. After 15 minutes, you can remove the heat and place the total boxes of crops on the floor. Psychedelic mushrooms remain sensitive to CONTACT: laziness, but not as fragile as before.

Step 13: remove the colonized material from the jar and mix it under the handle prepared in the breeding box. Make sure you do it quickly and don't keep the box longer than necessary.

Step 14: place the box at 24 ° C when the PsilocybeCubensis species grow like Psilocybin mushrooms; Check daily that the housing is very wet and that the vehicle is always submerged in water. When you notice it humidity does not regulate, spray it with distilled water. Remember that the bathroom water already contains unwanted guests, irrigation also depends on the quality of the water in your area, which can wreak havoc in a fully colonized box.

Step 15: After a few days, the Psilocybin mushrooms have colonized the media in a box, then they begin to form parts of the mushrooms for which you love them. When they reach about half the redness and reach the size where the hat is about to open soon, you can pick them up.

Step 16: Collect the Psilocybin mushrooms from the ground level and turn them gently so that they remain almost alone and do not pull hard. When finished, respray the box with water until the support gets wet again. The next rinse will arrive within two days, after which you will be ready to withdraw within one week.

How to collect Psilocybin mushrooms

In most cases, it is tough to determine when it is possible to collect mushrooms in a culture kit. Sometimes it's a lot easier if all the mushrooms are the same size, and you can pick them all at once, but that's never the case. A common mistake many people make is to remove large button mushrooms, so that small and medium-sized mushrooms continue to grow. This unknown mistake of many mushroom growers does not increase yield and also threatens to contaminate their culture kit.

The best time to pick Psilocybin mushrooms

One of the most important questions about growing Psilocybin mushrooms is the best time to pick mushrooms. The best time to collect them is when the covers of your Psilocybin mushroom haven't fully opened and still have a nice round head. When the mushroom reaches its own maximum size, it will start to open in a few days. The round hat will be released from the tree and take the shape of a hat. When this happens, it shows that the mushrooms want to multiply and release their spores. These spores are under the hood. When this happens, the fungi under the eyelids will turn black due to the spores released. At this point, your mushroom loses its potency after releasing the spores. Besides, spores are harmful to the mycelium and do not develop fungi

Guide for the cultivation inside

WHAT I have to grow mushrooms: 24 "wide-mouthed" pots now intact and they use "Kerr" or "ball." If you don't have a big mouth, you can't get a one-piece cake ... - Hammer - Cloves - Tapas woodblock - Wild WBS cubes -1 with lid and lid with rubber - Cow fertilizer fertilizer" CMC, "if you no longer have poop for a cow, use 1⁄4 of vermiculite instead. - Vermiculite - Aluminum foil - 'Optional' hydrated lime / gypsum - Tyvek filters - Spray spray for 3 - 3% hydrogen peroxide 2 with '32 floz ' -2-IPA "Isopropyl Alcohol" 70% is fine. Pot-Trainer-Pressure "PC" -clean tote large enough to handle 24pint - Plate

Use “Mycelium Grow kit " as a first-timer or beginner This set of cultures is already prefabricated. Unpack, that is, what you will do, do it.

Day 1 Step 1: Fill it with cold tap water until the soil is completely covered and immersed in it.

Phase 2: Soak for 12 to 24 hours.

Step 3: soak overnight. The substrate can be left to rest in the water for about 20 hours. They recommended 12 to 24 hours.

Step 4: Next, the next step is to drain the water and insert it into the bag with which it arrived. But remember to remove all the water.

Step 5: Insert the kit in the package and seal it with clips. Place the staples on one end of the other period and the other end. When you have finished, keep the place neat and dry.

Day 2 Phase 6: fungal growth: after a day, you will notice that condensation forms in the mycelium culture kit. But nothing else will happen. Therefore, you should not wait long, because it is only the second day.

Day 3 of the mycelium culture kit You will notice that there is still condensation on the top of the culture kit, especially if you look closely. In other words, fungal growth is minimal. Above, you can see white material.

Day number 4 - Day number 6: you will notice that the condensation will remain there. And there are white spots. They are like small white spots of mushrooms. I don't know if you can see how clear it is.

Day number 8: The white spots of fungi are growing and I'm sure they will serve as a place where mushrooms grow. In other words, you will see more significant mushroom growth on this day.

Day number 10: You will start growing many more mushrooms around it. They're coming back each time smaller, and if you look carefully there, see some growth.

Day number 12: We also have an impending increase. You will have a headache if you look closely.

Day number 13: On this day, you can see that we have some action in the cultural complex.

Day number 17: In the last few days we have had a lot of work. Again placing the bag left in a more upright position. This is to give mushrooms more room to grow. And if you look closely, the mushrooms grow and begin to sprout. Besides, you will notice that moisture is necessary for optimal growth. You can also take the clips and look inside to get a better view of what's going on. --

Day 20 of the mycelium culture kit on this day you will see that the mushrooms are blooming. That's all very lovely. It may not be much fuller and, if you look, you will see that the surface of the set is not 100% full. You can remove the bag. The mushroom picking will be ready between 24 and 48 hours. To collect, pick them up and put them on a paper napkin, and you'll be lying down. Finally, the whole process of breeding mushrooms helps to establish that the cultivation of mycelium took about 20-21 days in total.

- Another easy way to grow mushrooms indoors.

Here are a reliable and friendly way and the easiest way to grow mushrooms at home. This isn't necessarily the most automated or the most effective, but it's the simplest and most likely to succeed. Of course, this uses sterilized wheat bags that will be inoculated and allow for colonization. After they have been wholly colonized, divide them again so that the grain flows freely, and then prepare the substrate in bulk. Its most substantial substrate may be something pure pinworm small coconut - culture or a mixture of the two. You can also use a combination of manure and straw, but since it's more for your first growth, I recommend buying an only coconut, vermiculite or a mixture of both. This is because it has the lowest risk of contamination, and the yield is relatively high. Besides, it is recommended to use a high volumetric substrate generation factor. So, all you have to do (you don't have to do it according to sterile procedures) is to get yourself a plastic container. You can use a 64-litre box, and what they will do will be open bags of fully colonized cereals, add them to the container and then add bulk support. After adding the free base, mix the beans well. You can use your bare hands. I advise you to wash your hands. But again, this procedure doesn't have to be sterile so that you can work outdoors with your bare hands. After mixing and flattening, it should be about 4 inches deep. Although it is possible to administer a lower cost, it is not advisable to go more because there are simply no benefits. And for a pound, you'll end up collecting fewer mushrooms. After mixing and flattening, all you have to do is put the lid on, tightly hold and leave until it turns completely white, ultimately settled. It will take from one week to two weeks, depending on several factors. Once fully colonized, what you want to do is remove the lid and change it from half an inch to an inch and expose it to light. Okay, even if you mix the substrate directly, but some don't recommend it.

Tap water is beautiful, although it may be better to use freshly boiled water as the elimination of chlorine will potentially kill all the bacteria and spores that they may have in the water, even if they are most needed. So when you break the lid, mix it and expose it to light, put it in fruitful conditions. That's why you should start seeing and getting mushrooms in a week or two. You will have to mix it every day, and it is recommended to close it at night. Breaking the cap and move it sideways ensures ventilation and moisture sufficient need not worry further mixing several times a day. This is not a monotube. It requires more work. It has holes to fill the polyethylene on both sides, which regulate a better flow of air and humidity. It is more automated and more challenging to do. And if you are a manufacturer for the first time, you will probably see it every day, so it is not automation required.

This is very simple and probably the most natural way. It has better characteristics than PF teak. And if you consider costs and labor, your plastic bag only costs around $ 7 or more. Coconut or vermiculite can be obtained at a relatively low price, probably less than USD 10. The coconut can be purchased in most pet shops in brick. Plus, you can get vermiculite in most garden centers, as well as in places like Home Depot and Lowe's. One of the essential things about loose or coconut substrate is to make sure it is well hydrated. This means that you will immerse it for 24 hours and make sure it is full. The filling capacity is not water drops, but the push gently releases a few tears. So when you tighten it more, issue a small current. This is to ensure that the water does not sit on the container, which can cause various problems, such as going anaerobic and bringing CONTAM - inaction. However, this guarantees that there will be more water in the soil. This is one of the most critical factors that determine performance.

Coconut and vermiculite are not nutritious at all and are used only for their moisture content. You want to make sure he's well hydrated. Also, make sure it is purified. Simply add boiling coconut water and then dry. It will be redeemed. It is also AP - layers of vermiculite. Now let's follow the procedures, mix in general and see how it is.

✓First, add the pasteurized bulk medium. But you have to clean the container, rinse it and dry it. The substrate can be dissolved, for example, 5 pounds and colonized barn

✓ IS best for mixing as uniform as possible. It must be up to 4 inches.

✓ add another 5 kilograms of pasteurized coconut and vermiculite.

He has been properly hydrated. This is known as loose soil. To obtain a good measure, a faster colonization rate and higher yields, it is necessary to add another bag of colonized wheat to generate.

✓And still, mix it as thoroughly as possible. Make sure the seed is widely divided into individual pieces of grain, although it's okay if it's a little uneven.

✓It is recommended to break the grain so that it provides maximum inoculation - possible loosening points.

✓After mixing flatten the surface, making sure that everything is uniform and that it is not necessary to press. You want a light bulb and a spongy and light substrate.

✓ It can be up to 4 inches or too much. It's a little challenging to measure, but it's not so important to be so precise. You can only use 2 inches or just over 4 inches.

✓ Fill the lid and let it rest. It will colonize very quickly. You will see growth in two days. All small veins will become soft swabs and merge into a uniform white mass of mycelium.

✓After completion simply opens the lid, put it to one side and start flattening.

✓When spraying, make sure you have excellent hands.

✓You can use a little gentleman because it produces a softer mist, which helps humidity. You do it from all sides, cover and make sure all surfaces are wet. You should probably do more. But that's all. Also, make sure it has light. Fog several times a day and the mushrooms should start growing. Finally, it is so simple, even if everyone always complicates it too much with monotubes that require a filling or creating fruit chambers for PF shotguns

Showcase. But there is no such complexity when it comes to high efficiency, low workload and a relatively inexpensive process. It's tough to beat, especially when it comes to your first growth. And continue to use a transparent substrate. You do not want to have straw and manure, as it does not significantly increase productivity, but increases work, preparation, costs and the risk of contamination compared to coconut or vermiculite.

Chapter 8 The Most Known Growth Methods Of Magic Mushrooms

Recommended Sources of Supply

Finished mushroom mycelium is often offered as a so-called grain or cereal brood. The fungus grows through the rye, wheat or other grain until the mycelium has spread all over the place. The grain brood is particularly easy to dose and colonizes the wood quite quickly. Inoculation dowels are untreated wooden dowels on which the particular type of mushroom was cultivated. Here, too, the mushroom mesh has visibly grown through the whole wood. Both variants are suitable for developing tree trunks.

Especially on the Internet - but now also in hardware stores and garden centers - ready-made psilocybin mushroom brood is also offered, especially for growing on tree trunks. Here we present some German sources of supply.

The mushroom parcel has been sending various types of mushrooms as a brood from Nuremberg for several years. Besides, the mycelia can be purchased locally in the city.

Mushrooms & Equipment Shop, based in Münsterland, has been offering a wide variety of types for hobby growers and commercial cultivation since 2013. Vaccination dowels and cereal broods are available here.

Mushroom male from Saxony produces grain brood and inoculation dowels in organic quality. Cultivation packages are now also available in the Dehner Garden Center Pilz Wald - The Pilzmanufaktur based in Cologne offers in its online shop numerous types of mushrooms for the cultivation of tree trunks inoculated wooden dowels.

Inoculating the Wood

Depending on the type of inoculation, you need the following materials to inoculate the tree trunk:

- A chainsaw
- A wood drill
- A drill or a cordless screwdriver
- A hammer
- Foil or tape

- The respective mushroom brood

For the so-called dowel inoculation with mixed mushroom dowels, holes with a diameter of about eight millimeters are drilled into the trunk in the prepared trunk with the drill. However, they should not be more profound than inoculation plugs. The dowels are then carefully hammered into the hole with a hammer.

With the borehole method, you need a wood drill with a drilling diameter of about 20 millimeters and a grain brood. The advantage is that this type of mushroom brood spreads faster and more safely in the trunk than the mushroom dowel brood. After drilling the holes, fill the mushroom brood with a pestle and compact it slightly - the future mushroom stem is ready.

The cut vaccination method requires longer trunks by one meter. Here, the log is sawed two or three times over the entire length from below or above. Then you wrap the whole area with adhesive tape. You can also staple the tape for a better grip. To fill in the grain brood, cut a small window into the adhesive tape, carefully fill in the grain brood and compact it a little.

Finally, the inoculated trunk is wrapped in transparent film and then generously perforated with a nail or the like. This step is essential so that the stem retains enough moisture for the fungus and is supplied with oxygen at the same time. Alternatively, the trunks can also be stored under a plastic tarpaulin, but the humidity must be checked more often here. Store logs

Freshly inoculated wood is not yet hardy as long as the fungus has not been able to grow through the trunk ultimately. At 10 to 25 ° C, depending on the type of mushroom, it takes two to six months until the fungus has settled in its new living space. During this time, the trunk is best stored in the dark and checked for moisture now and then. If mold grows superficially on the wood, the log is too wet, or the ventilation is insufficient. If you put the trunk in a more airy place, the unwanted fungal attack will disappear.

Set up Tree Trunks in the Garden

If the wood has wholly grown through, you can already see the mycelium of the fungus emerging around the injection site. Now is the ideal time to remove the film or tape and set up the wood in the garden. Except for the Shiitake, all of the species mentioned require contact with the earth to form fruiting bodies. In order to do this, the trunks are buried in a shady spot a third to half in the ground. This type of cultivation is also called earth culture.

Shiitake cultures, on the other hand, do not need a substrate to grow: their trunks are leaned upright against a fence or wall -

this is also called aerial culture. Shiitake must be activated so that they form fruiting bodies correctly. First, the entire trunk is placed in cold water for 24 hours. Then you push it onto the ground three to four times, which promotes fruiting. Now patience is required because the trunks usually do not need any further care, but much time. On hot and dry days, however, the mushrooms enjoy a little water around and on the stem. Now it's time to show patience and wait for the first fruiting bodies. Because depending on the type of mushroom, it now takes a full 6 to 24 months before you can harvest for the first time.

Growing Psilocybin Mushrooms at Home

The psilocybin mushroom is gotten using mycelium, that is, the talus or nutrition mechanism of the fungi, which is constituted by a set of filaments or hyphae. The fertile part of the psilocybin mushroom is in the so-called hymenium, formed by sheets that are located in the lower part of the har. The mycelium contains the spores (in fungi they are called conidia) from which once grown, and they leave new fungi. It is acquired in blocks in specialized scores for its application, which is very simple. A further curiosity to know mushroom pickers in the field use net bags to introduce the specimens. While they walk looking for the mushrooms, they are released in the ground remains adhered to them, and in this way, scattering the mycelium that is to be used for the production of later crops.

Psilocybin mushroom cultivation is carried out in dark places (caves, basements, cellars, etc.), in bags or drawers built for this purpose. Appropriate measures of the drawers can be half a meter wide, a quarter meter high, and another quarter deep. As a substrate, we use a mixture that we have in the drawers in layers as follows:

- The first layer: first place a third of straw (preferably wheat, but also serves barley or oats).

- The second layer on the first layer, another third of pear is mixed with some sawdust. Another option is to use sandy soil.

- Third layer: technically, the whole ser is covered with well - shredded manure. Another option is to use cavalry manure.

Once the substrate has been layered in the drawers, we take the mycelium and crumble it over the last layer of manure. Then, we cover everything with a bit of peat and water, but not too much to prevent excess moisture from forming molds. From this moment, it is necessary to water frequently but not copiously, as already mentioned, preferably using a spray gun or watering-can, not a water jar. Psilocybin mushroom cultivation requires darkness (light kills them). We then place the drawers (they can be stacked on top of each other) in the cellar r basement that we have chosen. Taking care that there is always an absolute environmental humidity: The ideal for this crop is 80 %, which we can control using a hygrometer. Proper ventilation is also necessary. We must not allow the temperature to exceed 20° C.

Growing mushrooms at home is a job that anyone interested in increasing their food should try. Fungi are a healthy supplement in any diet since they have few calories and fat, are rich in fiber, and contain large amounts of potassium and selenium. Fungi grow better indoors, as it is easier to control light and temperature conditions. The most important thing to grow mushrooms is to learn to manage the requirements for their growth carefully.

Growing mushrooms is simple, and once they start dating, we can have continuous production until the nutrients in the preparation depleted. Even so, we have to take into account some previous considerations so that our crop not attacked by diseases that make our harvest unproductive.

Irrigation

When the growth phase, the fabric covering must be sprinkled with a water splash many periods a day. You continuously wet the soil but never mushrooms. It is fundamental to pay heed to water quality. Rainwater is safest, but mineral water must be used. Then it would be best if you sprayed the field like double times per day.

Psilocybin Mushroom Cultivation on Coffee Grounds

With a little patience and some coffee grounds, you can grow your mushrooms at home. We show everything about the procurement, care and harvest of the forest dwellers.

Coffee grounds falls in the trash or at least on the compost every day. It is still relatively unknown that the nutrient-rich leftover of the daily cup of coffee is also ideal for growing a wide variety of mushrooms. In the following, you learn everything about psilocybin mushroom cultivation on coffee grounds.

Psilocybin mushroom growing on coffee grounds

As starter as it may sound, you can also breed the funny forest dwellers in the kitchen. Below we show how to grow mushrooms on coffee grounds.

Coffee Grounds for Psilocybin Mushroom Growing

The nutrient-rich coffee grounds have recently been used more and more as a substrate for edible mushrooms, and ethical reasons. If we drink a cup of coffee, we consume just under one percent of the biomass of the original coffee bean. The rest remains as an excellent, warm-scented substrate. But instead of garbage, it should go into the bed and in the pots. Coffee grounds contain much nitrogen and can, therefore, be used not only for mushrooms but also for plants as fertilizer. The organic matter is also quickly and readily decomposed by small organisms in the soil and is then available to the plants. An article specifically about the use of coffee grounds as a plant fertilizer can be found here.

Another advantage for psilocybin mushroom cultivation is that the coffee grounds are freed of harmful microorganisms such as mold and bacteria by the hot brewing process. The coffee grounds of filter machines are particularly suitable for psilocybin mushroom cultivation. There are hardly any antifungal substances left, as is often the case with fresh beans. The leftovers from the self-grinding espresso machine are less suitable as a habitat for the mushrooms. The coffee grounds should not be older than two to three days old. Otherwise, the risk of mold infestation increases again. Freezing fresh sets largely prevents this, and so you can also build up a small stock.

How is a psilocybin mushroom built up?

The fungus itself is invisible to us most of the time because it lives in the ground and rarely dares to surface. In beautifully moist and nutrient-rich forest soils, a real network of mushroom cells, the so-called hyphae, forms under and between the roots of the trees. All cells taken together resemble a dense network of the most delicate roots and are called mycelium. The mushroom's mycelium communicates underground with neighbors and trees, digests organic matter and releases nutrients from the soil. When the conditions become humid, colder and darker - for example, in autumn - the psilocybin mushroom develops fruiting bodies. They then literally spring up like mushrooms and delight many animals and human collectors.

The umbrella-shaped or spherical fruiting bodies serve the mushroom mycelium only for reproduction. Above ground, thousands of spores are released for the next generation, and after a few weeks, the fungus itself is no longer visible. The mycelium meshes can grow into true giants and sometimes reach several tons in weight and many square kilometers. For psilocybin mushroom cultivation at home, the mycelium of the mushroom must be made to produce fruiting bodies.

Buy Psilocybin Mushroom Brood

At the beginning of your psilocybin mushroom cultivation, you need a little mycelium, which is usually on a small piece of wood or substrate. This dried, handy unit is also called mushroom brood or vaccine brood because it is used to "inoculate" the substrate with the mushroom and allow it to grow through. The starter mycelia are sold in various online shops, sometimes as streaky wooden dowels or loose in plastic bags. Mushroom growing sets with a finished substrate can, of course, also be fed with coffee grounds.

There are many different offers for growing your mushrooms on the Internet. But also in some garden centers, there are increasing sets for the most diverse types of fungi. We have selected some German sources of supply for you.

For several years now, psilocybin mushroom parcels have been sending various types of mushrooms out of Nuremberg, also as brood for breeding coffee grounds. Also, the mycelia can be purchased locally in the city.

Mushrooms & Equipment Shop, based in Münsterland, has been offering a wide variety of types for hobby growers and commercial cultivation since 2013.

Mushroom male from Saxony sends out certified organic mushroom substrates - especially for growing on coffee grounds. Cultivation packages are now also available in the Dehner Garden Center.

Chapter 9 Essential Magic Mushrooms Equipment

Pressure cooker

The pressure cooker is probably the most essential piece of equipment in your mushroom cultivation arsenal. You'll be using it regularly as an autoclave to sterilize substrates and equipment. You can buy them from grocery stores, second hand stores, scientific shops and mushroom supply stores. Both new and used models are advertised online.

The choice of make and size will depend largely on what you can afford, but there are some critical considerations to take into account:

Much of its use will be for sterilizing substrate in quart-sized mason jars. So buy one that's at least big enough to hold 6–10 jars.

It should preferably have a steam release valve or "stopcock" that you can control rather than a "rocker" type that automatically releases steam if the pressure goes above a certain level. The rocker type can lead to very rapid release of pressure and steam and is likely to cause anything liquid in the pot to boil up and overflow. This can be very messy and you can lose most of your material. What you really want is for the pressure and steam to reduce naturally once the pot has been removed from the heat source. This should take about an hour and a half. It must also retain a vacuum while it is cooling, so non-sterile air cannot get in to contaminate your cultures or substrate.

There must be an accurate dial to show internal pressure.

Buy from a reputable source. Look for models that have a minimum number of parts that can wear out–and where you can buy spares if you need to.

Pressure cookers can be very dangerous. They can explode if the pressure gets too high. They can implode if you pour cold water over them to cool them down. It is easy to scald yourself with the steam. So safety rule number one is to read the manual and know exactly how to operate your pot.

Make sure that it is working properly, with the lid properly sealed and locked into place. A bit of Vaseline on the rim will help to keep the lid sealed.

Use a basket inside the pot so that whatever you put into it doesn't touch any of the surfaces. You can make a basket, using galvanized steel wire. Stand the basket on a rack or trivet to keep it out of the water. Anything standing in water is not being sterilized as the pressurized steam cannot reach it.

There should be at least half an inch of water at the bottom of the pot. Some pots may give an amount in cups that should be used. Some of the water will evaporate in steam, and you want to be sure that there is enough left to maintain the pressure for the required period.

Depending on the heat source you are using, check to see whether your pot can be used on a gas burner or only on a stovetop.

Heat the pot slowly and let it cool down slowly. Doing this too fast can lead to the glass inside the pot shattering.

Let a full head of steam develop before you close the stopcock.

Never leave a pressure cooker unattended. Know how to operate the emergency release according to the manufacturer's manual.

Never put a sealed container into the pot. Make sure that there is a way for air to escape through the lid.

Finally, to ensure sterile conditions, wrap the outlet of the stopcock with an alcohol-soaked cloth prior to opening the valve. This will ensure that no spores or other contaminants enter the cooker when you vent the steam.

Most bacteria and other microorganisms are killed if you leave them in the pot for 15 minutes with the pressure at 15 PSI and the temperature at 121°C/250°F.

Alcohol lamp or mini torch

You will use the flame from these items for sterilizing equipment like inoculation loops and scalpels while you are working. Alcohol lamps are filled with rubbing alcohol and capped with a cotton wick and metal cap. Mini torches are generally butane-based. They are used by chefs and for soldering small items, so they are fairly easily available. They are easier to use if they have a base and can stand upright on the table top. Alcohol lamps can be found at scientific or mushroom supply shops.

Mason jars, lids and filter discs

These are three items, but are used together. You are going to use the jars to create spawn–ie the mixture of substrate and mycelium that can then be moved to other locations to propagate mushrooms.

You want plastic lids because you want your jar sealed, but air must be able to escape so that the jar does not explode in the pressure cooker. To modify them, cut or drill a 1-inch hole in the center. Then, fit the lid with a filter disk so air can enter, but harmful contaminants are blocked.

The filter disc is made of a synthetic fiber that can be sterilized and re-used. If they discolor from contact with substrate or mold spores, soak them in a quarter-strength bleach solution. You can buy the discs pre-cut to fit your lid, or make your own.

The pre-cut ones that are sold specifically for mushroom cultivation are very effective, with some being sold with the same specifications as HEPA air filters – i.e. 99,97% effective against microbes as small as 0.3 microns. They can be re-used multiple times.

For a cheaper option you might want to make your own using Tyvek–this is the material used for indestructible mailing envelopes. You can buy it in building supply stores. Just note that filters made from Tyvek should be cut larger than the lid and placed over the lid, not between the lid and the mouth of the jar. It must be tied down with elastic bands or the regular screw top outer band. Some people will place it between two lids that have had holes cut in them at the same position. The whole will meld into one piece once it has been heated in the pressure cooker. Use these discs only three or four times and then discard them.

Chapter 10 The Best Place To Grow Magic Mushrooms

If you feel like trying psilocybin mushroom cultivation yourself, you should be informed about the following aspects.

What Types Are Suitable?

There are various types of mushrooms, some of which feed on wood, leaves or semi-decomposed organic matter. Here you can find out which types also thrive on coffee grounds in your home.

'Oyster mushroom' (Pleurotus ostreatus)

These edible mushrooms grow in clusters from the substrate and form flat, depressed hats that are rolled up at the edges when young. They are available in the colors pigeon blue, grey, white and light brown. Because of their consistency, they are also called veal mushrooms. Their taste is excellent and mild and is therefore very suitable for soups, sauces and meat dishes.

'Lemon mushroom'/'Lemon yellow mushroom' (Pleurotus citrinopileatus)

Light yellow edible mushroom, which is closely related to the oyster mushrooms, which can also be seen in the shape of the fruiting bodies. The taste is strongly reminiscent of lemon, which makes it very interesting as a side dish with fish or salads.

'Roseseitling' (Pleurotus jammer)

Because of its soft pink color, it is also known as the flamingo mushroom. The mushroom is related to the oyster mushrooms and has a fan-shaped, lamellar fruit body with a velvety surface and a delicate mushroom taste — versatile use.

'Shiitake' (Lentinula edodes)

A fawn-colored edible mushroom with light flakes on a round hat and light brown-whitish stem, which is very popular in Asian cuisine due to its umami taste. Suitable for all kinds of dishes.

'Pioppino'/'Südlicher Ackerling' (Agrocybe cylindracea)

Brown-capped, medium-sized edible mushroom with white stem, which occurs naturally on poplar trees. It has a nutty, chestnut-like taste with firm flesh and can be used in a similar way to wild mushrooms.

Location And Climate For Psilocybin Mushroom Growing

Cool places with around 10 to 15 ° C and the highest possible humidity are particularly suitable for the cultivation of edible mushrooms. Mushrooms feel particularly comfortable in a mini greenhouse. Direct sunlight should be avoided, as should drying out the substrate. Mushrooms need some light, but for them to grow correctly, it only needs to be moderately bright. If the substrate is at the window, you have to make sure that there are no drafts, because the fungi cannot tolerate this at all.

Growing Psilocybin Mushroom on Tree Trunks

Shady places in the garden are ideal locations for growing mushrooms on tree trunks. Here you will learn how to grow delicious mushrooms close to nature.

Whoever owns a garden and has to remove a tree now and then often does not know where to put the wood. With the cultivation of mushrooms on tree trunks, the tree is used ideally and easy to care for. Here you will learn how to grow fresh mushrooms on the doorstep without much effort and over several years. Grow mushrooms on tree trunks

The cultivation of mushrooms on wood is the most original and natural form of psilocybin mushroom cultivation and was developed thousands of years ago in Southeast Asia - especially in Japan and China. Shiitake mushrooms (Lentinula edodes) were brought as exclusive gifts to the kings and emperors of the country. The use of mushrooms still plays an essential role in traditional Chinese medicine, and medicinal mushrooms on tree trunks were also cultivated early on. We have put together for you how you can grow mushrooms with wood in your garden.

The Right Wood for Growing Psilocybin Mushroom

Most mushrooms prefer to grow on hardwoods such as beech, oak and birch, as well as on all fruitwoods. They mainly feed on cellulose and lignin, the substances that make wood so hard and robust. Over time, they decompose even the thickest trunks and recycle the deadwood into organic matter. However, conifers have viscous, sticky resins that most edible mushrooms prefer to avoid. The exception is the smoky- leaved sulfur head (Hypholoma capnoides), which particularly likes to populate spruce and less often pine and silver fir.

The wood for the mushroom trunks should be cut as freshly as possible and then stored for at least two, but not longer than four months. The trunk diameter of the wood should be about 20 to 30 centimeters, and the length should be about 50 to 100 centimeters. Otherwise, the trunk will dry out too quickly. A stem with a diameter of 10 to 15 centimeters is sufficient for shiitake. The bark should be as undamaged as possible because later, it keeps the moisture better in the wood. The trunk is now watered for two to three days, whereby it should be covered entirely with water.

Habitats

The main types of habitats are:

- Pastures, meadows, or pastures
- Estercoleros

- Banks, gardens and lands removed (rubble)
- Forests

Grasslands or Pastures

This is a typical habitat of humid areas and low altitude. Here appears a large part of the species with a conical hat and thin foot/stem, such as Psilocybe semilanceata, Ps. Mexican, Ps. strictipes and others.

Estercoleros

These are species that grow directly on mammalian droppings. Therefore, there is no need to give great explanations. There are species of animals that are more favourable, such as cattle and horses, but even on elephant droppings, Psilocybes appear.

In this type of habitat, there are both psychoactive fungi (Psilocybe cubensis and Panaeoulus cyanescens), and non-psychoactive-fungi (Psilocybe coprophilia or Ps. Merdaria) and one of the main characteristics of it is its short life, which takes the stool to decompose.

They grow in gardens, riverbanks, and debris (removed lands), The gardens are an excellent place for the development of psycho-biblical species since they contain decomposing waste and materials. In manure-rich gardens, it is possible to find Panaeoulus subbalteatus in temperate zones and Panaeoulus cyanescens in tropical areas. Species may also appear as

Psilocybe cyanescens, Ps. stuntzii, Ps. Baeocystis, Ps. caerulescens and Ps. subaeruginous among others.

The riverbanks are open and sunny areas, so it is likely to find some of the species that occur in debris-removed lands. The appearance of fungi in these habitats is due to the floodwaters of the river, and the sediments that are deposited, with numerous wastes of trees or plants, are sandy.

A reasonably potent species that appears in this habitat is Psilocybe azurescens, a species discovered by the psilocycological sage, Paul Stamets.

The dumps or rather the removed lands are a habitat where it will be quite natural for us to find some species of Psilocybe. Some examples can be recent works of roads or highways that are built-in forests or similar areas, also an area of recent construction with its consequent earthworks, as well as landslides and natural landslides due to rain or other causes.

Forest

This category is the one that includes the most significant number of species of all those described above. Although due to the considerable variation of parameters, altitude, humidity, and rainfall that exists, each area will have its small catalogue of fungi, among which we will find some Psilocybes.

Perhaps where it is easier to find them is in the forest of certain conifers or deciduous trees (which produce litter and decomposition of it) such as poplar, willow, alder, and others.

Psychoactive mushrooms in Spain: there are eight recognized species of the genus psilocybe in Spain. It is quite probably and even sure there are more species, or some user knows them, but their existence is "officially" unknown.

As hallucinogenic, only three species stand out:

Psilocybe Semilanceata

The queen of the psilocybes is a species quite dominant and highly distributed throughout the globe.

Psilocybe Hispanica

Species endemic to the Pyrenean region (both on the Spanish and French side), were recently discovered by a Spanish researcher (Ignacio Seral-Bozal). It is a coprophile species - that grows directly on the shit or the manure - relatively strange since it grows between 1,500 and 2,300 m of altitude and develops even with very low temperatures or snow.

Psilocybe Gallaeciae

Species of recent discovery. At the moment, it is only known in Galicia (Northwest of Spain) and belongs to the Mexican section, being very similar to this, and it is the first species of this section that was discovered in Europe.

Other psychoactive species

There are several more species of Psilocybe, but they have not been shown to have psychoactive properties, or there is no conclusive data on the content of alkaloids or active ingredients that drive us to think on the possibility of an entheogenic use of that species.

It is also quite probable, by some references, that several Panaeoulus (Panaeolus subbalteatus) and Psilocybes can be found on the Iberian Peninsula as Psilocybe strictipes, Ps. cyanescens.

Chapter 11 The Cloning Procedure

Lucky for us, cloning mushrooms is not nearly as complicated as cloning mammalian cells. The process is fairly straightforward and can be done at home, which is great news for you!

Have you grown the perfect mushroom? Or a new strain that you wish to keep and continue experimenting with? Then you should clone it.

Spores have a variety of types of mushrooms that can grow from them, whereas when you use a clone, you are limiting the new fruits that will grow to be perfect copies of that specific mushroom type and strain (Shields, 2018).

Why Clone Mushrooms?

What and how to clone:

1. Clone unfamiliar or wild strains. Wild fruits are often either hard to grow commercially, or may just be unfamiliar to you. Cloning allows you to copy these mushrooms for study (do not eat wild mushrooms unless you are 100% sure of what it is you are eating) and, perhaps, cultivation.
2. Isolating and copying valuable traits. Cloning allows you to copy mushrooms that have desired traits, such as coloring, potency, or a new type of variant that you painstakingly cultivated yourself and wish to keep.

3. Clone your own harvest (or sometimes store bought fruits).

There are several reasons for cloning mushrooms.

You could, in theory, go out and hunt some wild mushrooms, and collect their spores for commercial cultivation. However, since growing from spores is largely a gamble as to the variety you would be getting (genetics, and a bit of luck, may you do end up with what you want, but that is incredibly rare), cloning can be used instead to make a direct copy from the mother fungus.

Cloning mushroom strains from the wild fruits allows you to cultivate and directly copy the variety and strain that you took the sample from.

The mushroom will most likely already be adapted to the environment from which the sample is harvested, making growth that much simpler. Especially if it was harvested from and will be cultivated outdoors.

Identify which characteristics you find desirable, such as potency level, coloring, size, or shape of the resulting fruits, and capture them with a clone.

Cloning will let you basically "copy and paste" these for yourself and future harvests.

The Cloning Process

The process involved in cloning is very simple.

You harvest a piece of tissue from the fruit you wish to clone, place it in an agar medium, and leave it to grow.

Yes, it really is that simple.

True, there are some caveats, but I will discuss these below.

While it is simple, the sample is still susceptible to contamination and infection. Therefore, before you dive right in, it is time to sterilize.

Wash your hands, don your gloves, and wear your mask. The safety procedures are not just for the health of your mushrooms, remember that. You do not want to inhale spores accidentally.

You can clone from any type of mushroom, whether it is wild, home-grown, or even store-bought. The process remains the same.

This works because the whole mushroom is still part of the living, breathing specimen. It does not simply die after being harvested and is still willing, and able, to continue growing and producing mycelium. Agar is the nutrient base which your sample will feed off of (the same way your mushrooms use substrate to grow). By placing these samples in the agar, the cells will be stimulated once again to grow. New mycelium will colonize on the agar plate.

Cloning, in a way, guarantees that your newly grown culture will contain the same genetic imprint as the mushroom the sample was taken from.

Harvesting Tissue

While you can select tissue from anywhere on the mushroom that you have harvested, the ideal place to cut your cloning sample from is as close as possible to the stem butt. They contain the better part of the reproductive cells, most likely due to the fact that they contain remnants of actual mycelium. You can harvest from the cap or other parts of the stem as well. While the stem butt gives you a higher chance of better production, it is also more prone to contamination as it grows much closer to the substrate that could potentially already be contaminated.

Note, however, that you should not harvest your sample from the gills. Gills contain spores, and you are trying to avoid spores (on account of you cloning your mushroom).

If you are up for an experiment, you can harvest gill tissue and place that in the agar, and see what springs up. For the purpose of cloning an identical mushroom, avoid the gills.

The cleanest sample can be found inside the stem, even if tissue from this location grows slower than the cells found in the area directly under the gills. You do not need a very large sample size. You can think of it as removing the core of the stem much like you would remove the core of an apple. That entire core can be subdivided to be distributed across several agar plates.

How To Clone

First things first. Select the fruit you wish to clone. A larger specimen is a better choice since you want a nice, large piece of tissue to work with for your sample.

Then sanitize the outer surface of the mushroom. Wipe down your mushroom thoroughly with some alcohol. This will render the mushroom inedible and unfit for consumption. While sanitizing the outer surface does not eliminate the risk of contamination, it does reduce the risk of bacterial growth significantly.

Step one: Tear the Fruit in Half

Tearing will leave you with the possibility of an uneven split, but it negates the possibility of introducing contaminants that could be transferred via the blade. You do not need to, but you can make use of a still air box. If you are using a laminar flow hood, keep in mind that you should hold your mushroom out of direct airflow. The inner part of the mushroom is naturally uncontaminated and contains fertile reproductive cells.

Step two: Transfer

Sterilize your cutting equipment. In this case, you will be using a scalpel, as this makes for accurate cutting and sample harvesting. You can sterilize the scalpel with a butane or propane torch.

Ensure that the scalpel is cool, however, when slicing into the mushroom. You do not want the heat to kill the viable tissue. The best place to harvest tissue from is in the fleshiest, thickest part of the mushroom. Either the center of the cap or the center of the stem. However, this will depend largely on the variety of mushroom you choose to harvest from.

You can either slice a small square about an eighth of an inch or run your blade cross-hatched across the surface of the inner part of the mushroom.

Place your sliver on your agar plate. Work as fast as possible, seeing as your agar dish should be left exposed to the open air as little as possible.

Some prefer to use a few slivers of tissue, to ensure the best possible result. However, since your slivers could contain contaminants, I would recommend one piece per plate. This is not necessarily the cheapest option, as agar can become expensive, but it reduces the chance of cross-contamination between pieces.

Cover your plates in parafilm or a similar covering to seal them. You can also use micropore tape.

Step three: Colonize

Once the agar plates have been wrapped, you can add another layer of protection in the form of a resealable plastic bag. It keeps dust (carrying other airborne contaminants) from settling on top of your agar dishes. Keep them at room temperature, and away from direct sunlight.

Within a few days, you will start to see the white growth of mycelium on the plates. It is still possible to get lucky on your first try and grow a clean, healthy mycelium. Keep an eye on your plates, the growth should not be any other color as this indicates foreign contamination. The risk is especially higher with wild mushrooms.

Should your plate appear overly populated with contaminants and you cannot see any salvageable white mycelium, toss your plate. If you can see untouched mycelium, you can transfer it to a clean plate of agar. Repeating the process could potentially yield a completely clean plate with a healthy mycelium that you can work with.

You can save a strain of mushroom that has the desirable characteristics you would like to continue working with through cloning in this manner.

Cloning is an incredibly helpful skill for the experienced, as well as beginner mycologist. Whether you use it for capturing new strains or just saving a copy of a strain you particularly like, cloning is fun and effective (Shields, 2018).

Chapter 12 How To Prevent Mushrooms Contamination

Types Of Contaminating Mushrooms

Penicillin is the most common type of mold in the world. Penicillin spores spread in the air and can easily contaminate your substrate. The mold then propagates into the can, expanding rapidly to infect the entire mycelium of the mushrooms.

Penicillin contamination is initially white in color and can be difficult to distinguish from the normal mycelium of fungi. Penicillin colonies have a circular shape. Penicillin often develops on wood. Precisely, for this reason, you should never use wooden supports or trays during mushroom cultivation.

Fortunately, Penicillio rarely contaminates the spores to inoculate. In most cases, contamination occurs on grain that has not yet been colonized. Penicillin gives off a smell of mold and dirt.

Aspergillus (A. Flavus, A. Niger, A. Fumigatus, A. Versicolor)

The Aspergillus fungus is another very common fungus that spreads through the air and can infect your cultivation. The Aspergillus mycelium has a light gray color, very similar to the mycelium of hallucinogenic mushrooms. Some Aspergillus species may be yellow, black, green, brown, or blue. There versicolor can take on multiple shades. Sometimes, Aspergillus colonies form a ring, with a thicker layer of mycelium at the edges. Aspergillus has a slimy, musty smell.

Trichoderma (T. Viride, T. harzianum, T. Koningii)

Just like Penicillio and Aspergillus, Trichoderma is a very common contaminating fungus. It is a particularly aggressive species, responsible for the destruction of countless crops. The Trichoderma mycelium takes on a greyish tinge, not always easy to spot. Spores can transfer to the substrate via contaminated soil, dust, or clothing. When the infection is already in place, a dense white layer appears on the surface. Trichoderma spores can produce a yellowish or green mycelium, and the colony is bounded by a whitish ring.

A Trichoderma contamination can occur at any stage of cultivation. Unfortunately, it can be difficult to notice the infection promptly, since sporulation can occur later, after inoculation. This is why mushroom growers should control the odor emanating from the mycelium, to detect the presence of mold and prevent it from spreading. Unfortunately, not all types of Trichoderma fungi have a characteristic odor. Some, however, emit an aroma similar to that of coconut.

Bacillus (B. Subtilis, B. Cereus)

Bacillus is not a fungus, but a type of bacterium. It is, however, a very dangerous and common contaminant in mushroom cultivation. B.subtilis, heat resistant, is the most widespread species. The presence of this bacterium manifests itself with a sort of crust or muddy area on the substrate. Contamination occurs mainly due to inadequately sterilized equipment. The risk of infection is greater when inoculation syringes are stored at higher than environmental temperatures. You can identify the Bacillus contamination thanks to the disgusting smell of rot emitted by this bacterium.

Mucor (Cat Hair)

The "cat's hair" mold is so-called because of its thin filaments (sporophores), with small heads on the ends. It is a contaminating mold that can attack the spores of inoculated fungi, but rarely develops on the substrate.

Rhizopus (R. Stolonifera, R. Oryzae)

Rhizopus is another contaminant. It is a very difficult mold to manage because it can spread very quickly. It has a similar appearance to "cat hair" mold, with long hair-like filaments, with a rounded tip. Rhizopus has an acrid smell, which sometimes resembles that of alcohol.

Fusarium

The Fusarium mycelium can easily be confused with that of hallucinogenic mushrooms because it has the same whitish color and grows at the same speed. The Fusarium, however, develops a brighter and brighter color, which, after a couple of weeks, can become pink, purple, orange or yellow. Often the Fusarium spreads in the mycelium due to inadequate sterilization of the work tools, and it can also contaminate the cans used in the PF technique.

Yeasts

Yeasts are another very common contaminant and, like fungi and bacteria, can destroy an entire crop. The presence of yeasts occurs with small spots inside the vase, usually yellow or white. Some types of yeast may resemble bacterial contamination. Yeasts usually do not attack substrates, but may be present in the spores to be inoculated. Yeasts give off various odors.

The basic rule is to always operate in a sterilized atmosphere and follow strict hygiene protocols if you want to grow mushrooms successfully, preventing harmful contamination. Only one noxious spore or bacteria is necessary in most cases to contaminate the entire production of mushrooms. Normally, in a 100% sterile environment, such as a laboratory, hobby growers do not function. Nonetheless, several measures are in place to minimize the risk of pollution.

How To Avoid Contaminating Mushrooms

Sterile Cultivation Environment

Some pollutants are released into the atmosphere, such as molds and fungi. They can be anywhere, and you can't see them, even in relatively clean places. It can, therefore, be difficult to remove these toxic molecules. Researchers use specially filtered air cabins called laminar flow hoods in professional laboratories. This particular equipment is, sadly, very costly, and definitely beyond the scope of an occasional mushroom grower. But, if you love DIY, on the other hand, you might be able to build a semi-professional laminar flow hood.

Sterilize Substrate and Wheat

Airborne compounds that contaminate the mushrooms are a major problem. But they are often already present in the soil as well. Most substrates and loose grains contain harmful species that must be extracted or at least reduced prior to use. Before inoculating the spores of the fungus, you must sterilize both the substratum and the seed.

Using a pressure cooker that is large enough to hold all the stuff, you may sterilize sawdust blocks and wheat grains. Place the block of sawdust in the pot and sterilize for about 2 hours and a half. For wheat, it will be enough to do it for 1 hour and a half.

Sterilization is a procedure that removes all types of bacteria. Pasteurization is another method that uses heat to remove most bacteria. Pasteurization is not adequate to sanitize sawdust blocks, but it is a valid technique if you use straw as a substrate. To pasteurize the straw, heat it at 65–82 ° C for at least an hour and a half. Some growers put the straw in a pan full of water, and then heat it up on a stove.

Try To Stay Clean While Working With Mushrooms

We now know the factors that may contaminate the atmosphere, the soil, and the surface. But the main source of pollution we have not yet considered: yourself!

Your clothes, body, and hair can serve as contaminant vectors. Personal hygiene is important to grow mushrooms in the best possible conditions.

Take a shower and wash your hair before you focus on your mushrooms. It's not a short shower we're talking about. Rub the skin well, wash thoroughly in every area of the body, even under the nails and behind the ears. To kill bacteria on the body, hand sanitizing items can be very useful.

In professional laboratories, operators wear a white coat. You probably won't have such a sterilized uniform available, but you should still use clean clothes before you start working on your cultivation. It is advisable to also wear a mask.

Use Sterilized Instruments

Obviously, it makes no sense to work in a perfectly clean environment if sterilized instruments are not used. In other words, you need to sanitize all equipment and tools, such as scalpels, blades, and syringes.

When using the scalpel for transfers, you must remember to sterilize it. To do this, heat it over a flame for about 30 seconds until it turns red. You can use a Bunsen burner or an alcohol lamp. If you have nothing else available, a lighter is also fine.

Clearly, you cannot heat the syringes and plastic instruments over a flame. In this case, you must use alcohol to sterilize them.

Alcohol is also useful for cleaning all surfaces, including cans and bags. A couple of bottles of denatured alcohol (isopropyl) and a few sheets of blotting paper will allow you to keep your workspace clean and disinfected.

Chapter 13 Legal Risks

A judge acquitted a Mediterranean shopkeeper who sold "bags of smell" because the judge understood that they were NOT for consumption since Psilocybe Cubensis mushrooms were inside a bag of machine-sewn cloth, and with a label that said: "Just to be smelled". Several hemp shopkeepers (grow shops) was acquitted despite having psilocybin in their stores, stating that they were mushrooms for their consumption and it was found that they had a small number of fungi.

(Smell Bags. Pedro Caldentey, 2008. Hemp No. 122 February, p. 18)

On the other hand, another judge sentenced Vincent, from the quick shop "Marcha Shop" (Seville) to 4 years in jail, because he sold freshly packed mushrooms with an expiration date. And although his defense lawyer, Mr. Enrique Lerchundi, invoked the official communiqués of the INCB (International Narcotics Control Board) that leave mushrooms, herbs and potions out of international control, it was no use. The judge condemned him based on the article of the Spanish Criminal Code that prohibits in addition to pure substances, "any preparation containing them". And according to the judge, fresh mushrooms vacuum packed with an expiration date were undoubtedly a "preparation".

Psilocybe mushrooms were not included in the list of prohibited drugs, such as Cannabis, coca leaves or Opium Poppy.

It is possible that the arrests so far have been a strict follow-up of the Spanish Government to the recommendations of the INCB, for the moment conclude that international treaties and INCB reports are minimum documents. From there onwards, each country decides whether to repress more, but never less.

Are Spores Legal?

Yes, the spores are legal.

According to Alacannabis's lawyer, regarding spores he wrote in 2005:

"A priori, it would not involve the sale of spores, or bread, any criminal or administrative punishment covered by the Medication Law (...) technically it is possible to sell both spores and fungal bread. All this with the risk of suffering some action of the dull administration. In some cases, the bread was not even intervened, and in others, the people who were intervened have been acquitted".

(Legal Regime of the Hallucinogenic Fungi. Héctor Brotons in the free newspaper "Soft Secrets". December 2005; p. 29).

The legal situation seems quite confusing. The Spanish Administration, so far, has followed a clear prohibitionist trend. "Psilocybin and psilocin", Eduardo continues, "the psychoactive principles of fungi, are considered drugs for all purposes". Traffic, cultivation, production or promotion of its consumption constitute a crime.

On the other hand, the possession of fresh mushrooms would be legal, while if they are dry, powdered, bagged or encapsulated, it would be penalized. Anyway, it depends a lot on the quantities: a few dried mushrooms could be justified as intended for own consumption, and a large amount of them in the new State would surely be understood as designed for traffic. The same goes for self-cultivation. It all depends on the amounts and the assessment of the judge.

Draws attention to the surprising variety of mushroom consumers that exists. At first sight, it is difficult to think that HR, a conservative-looking thirty-year-old lawyer who prefers to maintain his identity in anonymity, has psychedelic hobbies. Chairing the living room of his house in the bad Madrid neighbourhood of Salamanca, there are four grow-kits of Stropharia Cubensis, the most popular of hallucinogenic mushrooms. "I have been fond of fungi for a long time, in general, and hallucinogens, in particular", he says. "The cultivation begins with the spores, which are, as it were, a kind of seed. To get a fungus to be generated, they must be introduced into a soil prepared with organic materials. This process must be carried out under particular conditions of sterility, light, humidity and temperature so that bacteria don't attack it. It is not simple, and preparation is needed. On several occasions, I tried very carefully, but I always failed".

HR takes the issue of self-cultivation seriously: "Fortunately, about seven or eight years ago, a grow-kit began to be sold that includes a plastic pot with the spores already inoculated on the ground. This means that the most complicated part of the process is already done. Also, in the last two years, a new version has appeared with a semi-transparent bag that has an air filter that maintains the humidity conditions. In this more sophisticated model, mushrooms take two or three weeks to begin to leave from the mail, and a minimum of three crops are obtained.

I have managed to get up to seven. The most straightforward Stropharia Cubensis kits come from the Netherlands and are purchased online. They cost 50 e and produce 1/4 of a kilo of fresh mushrooms, which dry will be 25 grams and equal dose numbers. I get the feeling that an explosion is coming in the consumption of magic mushrooms". He remained silent for a few seconds before continuing: «I was introduced to this topic by a group of colleagues in their 40s. In their youth, they had been very fond of trips and had moved to mushrooms as who passes from tennis to paddle. Sometimes we organize dinners with this type of mushrooms when cooking as they do not lose their hallucinogenic properties».

International Boom Interestingly, globalization is having its hallucinogenic effects. Magic mushrooms are experiencing a boom in countries like the United Kingdom. A few days ago, The Guardian newspaper commented on the existence of Psyche Deli, a store in the famous Portobello market where they are openly traded. The business owners decided to contact the British Interior Ministry to know precisely what the legal situation was. An officer told them that dried mushrooms, or "altered by man", are considered illegal drugs, but that the cultivation and trade of fresh mushrooms are not prohibited, nor is grow-kits. The people of Psyche Deli immediately contacted producers in the Netherlands.

They estimate that they sell about 50 kilos of mushrooms a week, which is equivalent to 500 individual doses. To avoid problems with the law, they are not promoted as hallucinogens but as decorative elements or intended for mycological research. The groups fighting for the decriminalization of consumption have put their finger on the sore. As Steve Rolls, a spokesman for the Transform agency dedicated to this issue, said, "it is absurd that eating fresh mushrooms is legal, but if they are prepared in an infusion or a tea you can end up with 14 years in jail".

In Japan, the consumption of hallucinogenic mushrooms is also extended, taking advantage of legal gaps. "It's another example of how ridiculous drug legislation can be", continues Steve. Smoking marijuana there can carry a penalty of five years in jail, but there is no penalty for importing, buying or selling magic mushrooms. This happens because they are not classified as narcotics, but as poisonous plants, which means they are legal only if they are not sold for consumption. For this reason, they are offered as decorative elements to beautify Japanese homes.

Mystical trips It is interesting to briefly point out aspects of the ancestral culture associated with magic mushrooms. Dijo, pseudonym of Gabriel González, is a young artist who is dedicated to the development of virtual spaces. He has travelled on numerous occasions to the mountainous region of Oaxaca, in Mexico, where the mythical María Sabina lived.

In that place is Don Patricio, who guides him in his experiences with magic mushrooms. “This is an actual ritual that begins with the trip, and you have to get there, meet people. The whole family participates in mushroom making, from young children to grandparents. For them, it is a process of learning and healing. It is a ceremony that seeks inner knowledge: nothing to do with the idea of taking drugs to escape and have a good time”.

The elements for debate are served. “Just before the elections - says Xaquin, from the magazine Hemp - a bill was in progress that aimed to limit the trade of such dangerous plants like thyme or chamomile, and that, of course, included fungi. It is an apparent attempt to leave everything in the hands of large pharmaceutical companies. I get the feeling that, right now, self-cultivation is the most realistic alternative. On the other hand, the network has become the great centre for dissemination and exchange of information on hallucinogenic mushrooms. It is essential to get advice to avoid surprises".

What The Law Says

Legally, psilocybin and psilocin are considered drugs for all purposes.

Trafficking, cultivation, production or facilitation and promotion of its consumption constitute a crime against public health. Mushrooms are considered severely harmful to health, so the sentences for these crimes will go from 3 to 9 years in prison or 9 to 13 years if there are aggravating factors (selling in schools, to minors, etc.) The possession of small amounts destined for self-consumption is not considered a crime but can be punished with fines ranging from 300 to 3,000 Euros.

The property of fresh mushrooms would be legal, and that of dried, powdered, bagged or encapsulated mushrooms would be illegal. However, this also depends on the quantities: a few dried mushrooms could be justified as intended for own consumption, but a large number of fresh mushrooms would surely be understood as designed for traffic.

The possession and sale of spores are not considered a crime, insofar as they do not contain psilocybin or psilocin and therefore cannot be regarded as drugs. Even so, once the spores have given way to the appearance of the fungus, justice will understand that it is a drug.

Conclusion

Good Roll

- Laughter and some euphoria are typical of the early stages of the trip or with the use of low doses.
- Subsequently, the user usually goes into a state of calm and tranquility, accompanied by a marked sense of transparency and mental clarity, so marked that it is common that the new perspective from which things are seen is interpreted as a real revelation. Such revelations may refer to each person's scope or to metaphysical or religious issues that concern all of humanity or the entire universe.
- The perception of the world is disrupted: time slows down, the notion of past, present and future is directly accelerated or disappeared. The colors shine differently, the shapes are deformed, strange lights or sounds and visions are perceived with the eyes closed, until, with the use of high doses, you even see more with the eyes closed than open ("close your eyes, and you will see").
- All this can be lived as something fascinating, overwhelming mind, stunning and beautiful, and this can lead us to an emotional state of authentic satisfaction and gratification, a state that will often be

shared with the rest of the people present, being able to establish communication and emotional ties that are unusually intense.

Bad Roll

- However, the alteration of emotions, perceptions and thinking, will not always present a kind and funny face. What is perceived can entirely be lived as horrifying and distressing.
- The change of perspective in a way of thinking might well lead us to say something like: "I don't understand anything about this world". Mystical revelations could lead us to visit Hell instead of Heaven, just as metaphysical revelations could make us understand that not only are we are miserable, but so is all of humanity.
- In short, laughter could turn into tears and calm into panic and anxiety. It is not uncommon for the same trip to pass successively through both pleasant and distressing moments.
- Any change in the environment, in what we do or in what comes to mind, can redirect the experience in one way or another and make us go from fascination to horror or vice versa. For this reason, in the face of unpleasant sensations, one has the opportunity to redirect the trip to something more pleasant by

merely trying to think about other things, do something different or change the environment (music, site, etc.).

- However, sometimes (especially with high doses) this can be very difficult, and the person can be caught in a kind of vicious circle with recurring thoughts on the same subject ("I have gone crazy" or "they are persecuting me") who is unable to get out of his head. This is a "BAD TRIP”.
- Some believe that even a bad trip can be understood from a positive point of view since they affirm that from bad experiences, one can learn as much or more than from good ones. Moreover, there is less doubt that he is having a bad time and taking the positive side may not be so simple: it requires work, self-analysis and reflection (perhaps that is why many people do not want to hear or talk about bad trips).

The "Bad Trip"

How to make a wrong journey

If someone is having a bad trip, we must try to get the person (as if it were the case) to relax and calm down.

Please do not leave the person alone.

Never try to reassure him with slaps or another violent behaviour.

Don't whisper with other people in your presence or it could increase your paranoia.

If you intend to reassure someone, you must appear calm: no shouting, fuss or nervousness.

If you are in a noisy or crowded place, you should take the person to a less busy place.

You should talk slowly and respect the person's willingness to speak or keep silent.

You shouldn't force the person to speak or listen to you. You should tell them to breathe slowly and deeply, and if necessary, you should set the pace for them.

You should remind them they have consumed mushrooms and are having a bad trip that will diminish as the effects go away.

This may be enough for relatively mild bad trips.

Sometimes, however, the person will be impervious to any objective approach you propose ("it is because of the mushrooms, it will happen to you"), so it will be convenient to limit yourself to transmitting a sense of security: A hand on the shoulder, a jacket or a blanket that covers him, eyes closed, slow breathing, quiet music and only small phrases of support such as "let yourself be carried away by experience" or "move on". Because at this point, the only way out of the vicious circle of the bad trip is to give up and let go.

There will also be cases in which the anguish will not cease until the effects of the mushrooms have subsided. Especially then you will have to be patient and stay calm,

If the situation is complicated or the interested party requests it: Call Security!

Printed in Dunstable, United Kingdom

68685682R00080